SILK RIBBON MACHINE EMBROIDERY

Dedication and Many Thanks to:

My family, my husband, Ed, and children, Sarah and Adam, for their patience, support and understanding while Mom spent untold hours behind a sewing machine and computer keyboard.

My parents, Jerome and Esther, for recognizing a little girl's love of sewing and starting her along the path.

JoAnn Pugh-Gannon, Editor, mentor and friend, who believed in an unknown sewer's talents early on.

Fellow sewing writer, Jackie Dodson, who helped me realize that I could author a book.

Acknowledgements

No publishing effort is a sole venture. I would like to thank the following companies for their contributions in product and knowledge to help create the projects in this book.

Bernina of America, Bucilla Corporation, Clothilde, Inc., Chicago Historical Society, Dimensions, Inc., EZ International, Island Fibers, The Metropolitan Museum of Art, Ornamental Resources, The Singer Company, Sulky of America, Sweet Child of Mine, June Tailor, Inc., True Colors International, and the YLI Corporation.

Silk Ribbon Machine Embroidery

Nancy Bednar

Sterling Publishing Co., Inc.
New York

A STERLING/SEWING INFORMATION RESOURCES BOOK

Owner: JoAnn Pugh-Gannon
Photography: Kaz Ayukawa, K Graphics
Book Design and graphics: Rose Sheifer, Graphic Productions
Illustrations: Barbara Abrelat
Index: Anne Leach

Sewing Information Resources is a registered trademark of GANZ Inc.

Library of Congress Cataloging-in-Publication Data
Bednar, Nancy.
     Silk ribbon machine embroidery / Nancy Bednar.
        p.   cm. — (Great sewing projects series)
     Includes index.
     "A Sterling/Sewing Information Resources Book."
     ISBN 0-8069-9493-2
     1. Silk ribbon embroidery. 2. Embroidery, Machine. I. Title.
TT778.S64B43   1997
   746.44—dc21   96-52099
                                         CIP

A Sterling/Sewing Information Resources Book

10 9 8 7 6 5 4 3 2 1

First paperback edition published in 1998 by
Sterling Publishing Company, Inc.
387 Park Avenue South, New York, N.Y. 10016
© 1997 by Nancy Bednar
Distributed in Canada by Sterling Publishing
% Canadian Manda Group, One Atlantic Avenue, Suite 105
Toronto, Ontario, Canada M6K 3E7
Distributed in Great Britain and Europe by Cassell PLC
Wellington House, 125 Strand, London WC2R 0BB, England
Distributed in Australia by Capricorn Link (Australia) Pty Ltd.
P.O. Box 6651, Baulkham Hills, Business Centre, NSW 2153, Australia
Printed in Hong Kong
All rights reserved

Sterling ISBN 0-8069-9493-2 Trade
            0-8069-9492-4 Paper

TABLE OF CONTENTS

INTRODUCTION

My first introduction to silk ribbon embroidery was through my husband's and my love of antiques. Browsing through dusty antique shops or walking the aisles of convention hall shows, bits of beautiful and fragile ribbon embellishments appeared on vintage gowns and accessories. I was drawn to the visual riot of color and texture in Victorian crazy quilts where ribbon clusters could be spied tucked into the corners of the sewn patchwork pieces.

Before long, an occasional book or two surfaced in the sewing market on silk ribbon embroidery—all done by hand. These beautiful presentations of a long ago art, such as Judith Baker Montano's *Crazy Quilt Odyssey* or *Silk Ribbon Embroidery* were a visual treat for the eyes and a temptation for my not so nimble fingers. Memories flooded back to me of back porch afternoons spent with my patient grandmother trying to teach an all-thumbs granddaughter to hand stitch stamped pillowcases and dresser scarves. Dutifully, I'd dip into my cookie tin of embroidery flosses and needles, and unsuccessfully try to make my stitches as pretty and even as my Grandma's. I didn't. My salvation came when my mother sent me to an after-school park district sewing class where I discovered the sewing machine! My days with a hand needle were over!

Over the years, I joyfully created entire wardrobes for myself and everyone else in my family. Casual sewing led to commission work and teaching. While on the staff teaching at an heirloom school, I taught a class that was also learning to hand embroider a small silk ribbon project with another teacher.

After three hours of frustration, few were finished. When they returned after lunch for my class, all they wanted to do was machine sew, put the pedal to the metal—but fast! It was then that I realized that there are truly two different kinds of sewers, machine enthusiasts and those who love handwork. Occasionally these two groups cross over and people sew both ways, but not often. After my youthful experience with handwork, I knew where I belonged. I vowed, however, to find a way to blend traditional hand silk ribbon embroidery with machine techniques.

Silk Ribbon Machine Embroidery is the result of that vow. The purpose of this book is not to replace the beauty of handwork techniques, but to offer an alternative method to the sewing machine lover so that all can celebrate the beauty of ribbon embroidery. I encourage machine lovers to purchase hand technique books for inspiration and reference when planning a ribbon project by machine. Over the past two years, I have studied countless handwork books, both old and newly published, to learn how to adapt and recreate traditional ribbon stitches by using the sewing machine. Many of our built-in stitches, both decorative and utility take on new beauty when sewn in silk. Simple tacking, looping and twirls can replicate hand needlework basics. Sewers today spend considerable money to purchase sewing machines that include elaborate stitch packages. It's time to take a new look at those stitches and make your sewing machine earn its keep.

The techniques are simple, the results beautiful and the ribbons are luxurious. What better sewing situation could there be? Try some simple stitches and delight in your creativity. We knew you could do it all the time!

Nancy Bednar

Court presentation dress. Detail: ribbon flowers, front
hemline. Worn by Mrs. George Henry O'Neil for
presentation before George V in June, 1928. Designed by
Boué Soeurs. White net embroidered in silver cord over
pink chiffon trimmed with silk ribbon flowers.

 A HISTORICAL PERSPECTIVE

Tracing the elusive history of silk ribbon popularity throughout the years reveals a trail full of fits and starts. Early records mention ribbon embellishment worn by royalty and members of the French court as early as the mid 1700's.

Silk ribbon embellishment as a needle art did not develop significantly until the mid-Victorian era. Fashionable "ladies" magazines such as *Godey's Ladies Journal* uncovers various needlework techniques with a touch of ribbon embroidery here and there. This ribbon popularity culminates in the early 1900's with spectacular work done by Parisian dress houses.

Silk ribbon embroidery seemingly disappears until its present day revival. However, it's safe to assume that lovers of fine needlecraft, such as French hand sewing enthusiasts, have quietly been stitching ribbon fantasies all along. A brief history follows...

French Beginnings

Silk ribbon handwork can be sketchily traced as far back as the royal courts of the mid-to-late 1700's. Reserved exclusively for royalty and the wealthy gentry, the elaborately designed front pieces of ladies gowns offered an ideal location for ribbon embellishing. These ribbon decorations could be permanently sewn into a garment, or, arranged onto a backing and pinned on where desired. This way, a lady of the court could change the look of her gown by removing floral sprays and replacing them with others.

The popularity of ribbon-enhanced garments grew so much it traveled the English Channel where it soon became the style of choice for royalty and ladies of the British court, as well.

From Victorians to the Early 1900's

If you understand the Victorian mindset that "more is better," it is easy to appreciate the appeal of ribbon embellishment in the mid-1800s to early 1900s. Garment instructions advised adding ribbon motifs to key areas of dresses, such as collars, cuffs and waistlines. Already adept at needlework with many different threads, Victorian ladies easily replaced these fibers with ribbons to add extra flourishes to their already detail-laden garments. Ribbon embroidery was also suggested as additional embellishment on the popular "Crazy" quilts. The added dimension of ribbon stitches on top of thread work gave the stitcher a new tactile challenge and was a testimonial to her skill with a needle.

Ribbon embroidery was never more glamorous than when interpreted by the Parisian design house of Boué Soeurs. The 1928 gown pictured at the opening of this chapter beautifully illustrates their work. This court presentation dress consisted of an overdress and train made of oyster white net over chiffon, embroidered in silver with insets of silver blue lamé. The overdress front, sides and train are lavishly embroidered with elegant, multi-colored silk ribbon cascades.

Ribbon art in the 1920s was not restricted to garment usage. A popular needlework book of the day, *Old Fashioned Ribbon Art*, by Ribbon Art Publication Co., featured "clever, practical and dainty" ribbon projects for milady, baby, and the home. Ribbons were manipulated into accents on everything from hats to baby blankets to garters and lampshades.

Photograph courtesy of the Chicago Historical Society, Hope B. McCormick Costume Collection. Gift of Mr. Albert J. Beveridge III.

Bag of metallic, pale green brocade. Entire bag and handles embellished with silk ribbon flowers, lace and gold paillettes. Circa 1900.

Photograph courtesy of the Chicago Historical Society, Hope B. McCormick
Costume Collection. Indefinite loan from the Art Institute of Chicago,
donated by Mrs. Potter Palmer II.

Summer dress of black corded grenadine with pink and
green stripes over green taffeta. Leg-o' mutton sleeves and
skirt hem accented with ruche trim of pink and green
ribbons. Circa 1892, Paris.

Photograph courtesy of Chicago Historical Society, Hope B. McCormick Costume Collection. Gift of Mrs. Carl B. Davis.

Wide brimmed hat of blue-gray crepe with bias cut silk geometric ribbon trim on the brim. Knife pleated crown edged with pink picot edged band embellished with pastel ribbon flowers. Circa 1917.

Ribbon embroidery then quietly slumbered until our modern day revival. Thanks to today's talented and inspiring silk ribbon handwork artists, many stitchers are now exposed to and tempted by the beauty of silk ribbon stitching. Whether the design is produced by a hand needle or on a sewing machine, the graceful garlands of flowers, lovingly stitched, are available to all.

 GETTING STARTED...RIBBONS, THREADS, AND BEADS

Duplicating silk ribbon embroidery by machine draws upon many of the same supplies used by traditional hand stitchers. Silk or man-made ribbons, embroidery threads and beads are among the supplies shared by hand and machine embroiders alike. The following pages discuss the virtues of 100% silk versus ribbons made from man-made fibers, monotone vs. hand-dyed goods. Threads are suggested for background embroidery, plus beads and pearls to put extra sparkle in your work.

Silk Ribbons

Whether you are a dressmaker of long standing or new to sewing, the beauty and elegance of silk ribbons will soon have you under their spell. Soft and pliable with a subtle sheen, these ribbons are available in a variety of sizes and colorations. You'll quickly have a growing collection in your sewing room!

100% Silk or Man-made Fiber Look-alikes?

ALL-SILK RIBBONS

Woven silk ribbons, 100% bias cut, have been the traditional ribbon of choice for handwork for many years. Manufactured by the YLI Corporation and Bucilla Corporation, they are most commonly found in the 2mm, 4mm, 7mm, and 13 mm widths. The ribbons are either wound onto plastic spindles or spools, or carded in predetermined yardage. A larger width of 32mm is also available from YLI.

RIBBONS FROM MAN-MADE FIBERS

With the revival in popularity of silk ribbon work, manufacturers have created easy-care silk look-alikes from man-made or alternate fibers. These ribbons fray less and are available in rainbow or ombré striping. They are available in the traditional widths, in differing fiber contents and densities. Mokuba produces Heirloom Sylk™, a 100% Azlon™ product, while True Colors offers Silken™ ribbons, a 100% rayon product. Since some of the man-made fibers have textured surfaces, they are best saved for couching techniques, because they do not feed smoothly from the bobbin.

MONOTONE OR HAND-DYED?

Monotone silk ribbon is manufactured pre-dyed in a rainbow of colors. Ideal for beginners, the advantages of factory dyed silk goods are colorfastness (no color bleeding or run-off) and consistency of color from one package to another. Color matching during a project is assured.

Hand-dyed silk goods offer multiple color variations within one length of ribbon. Dyed in smaller quantities by independent studios, these ribbons can add subtle shading and visual interest to any silk ribbon project. Usually found in the traditional widths, an advantage of including hand-dyed ribbon in your embroidery is the color variations achieved using just one strand of ribbon, no snipping or changing necessary!

TEST FOR COLORFASTNESS

It's a good idea to test hand-dyed and deep-colored ribbons for dye run-off before using them. Bright or intensely colored darks may bleed onto your project. Even if a silk ribbon project ultimately will be dry cleaned, a burst of steam from an iron during final pressing may trigger some dye release from an untreated ribbon.

To test, immerse hand-dyed silk yardage in a clean glass of lukewarm water, allowing it to soak for 3-4 minutes. If the water becomes colored, empty the glass and refill. Soak and check for color run off again. Repeat the process until the water remains clear. Rinse a final time with cold water. **Note:** The color of the ribbon may lighten somewhat.

Ribbon Reference Chart

PRODUCT NAME AND MANUFACTURER	CONTENT	SIZES AND COLORS AVAILABLE (YARDAGES IN PACKAGES)	CARE RECOMMENDATIONS	COMMENTS
Silk Ribbon™ YLI Corp.	100% silk	2mm 86 colors (5 yds) 4mm 185 colors (5 yds) 7mm (5 yds)	Cold water wash, delicate cycle	Couch or bobbinwork; 13 mm and 32 mm available
Pure Silk Bucilla	100% silk	4mm 65 colors (3 yds) 7mm 39 colors (3 yds)	Handwash in mild dish detergent	Couch or bobbinwork; 13 mm available; silk organza available in four widths
Petals™ Sweet Child of Mine	100% silk Hand-dyed	4mm 60 colors (3 yds) 7mm 60 colors (3 yds)	Cold water wash, delicate cycle	Couch or bobbinwork; variety pack available
Elegance Ribbons™ Island Fibers	100% silk Hand-dyed	2mm 10 colors (3 yds) 4mm 44 colors (3 yds) 7mm 15 colors (3 yds)	Cold water wash, delicate cycle	Couch or bobbinwork; sampler pack available
Heirloom Sylk™ Mokuba	100% Azlon	2mm 24 colors (3 - 4 yds) 4mm 78 colors (3 yds) 7mm 26 colors (3 yds)	Normal wash, line dry	Couch or bobbinwork; organza and sparkle ribbons available

Embroidery Threads

Background embroidery of trailing vines and curlicues is a mainstay of most silk ribbon designs. I prefer to stitch these secondary elements in with a lighter look, using a variety of decorative threads.

Consider these threads teamed with your machine's utility or decorative embroidered stitches:

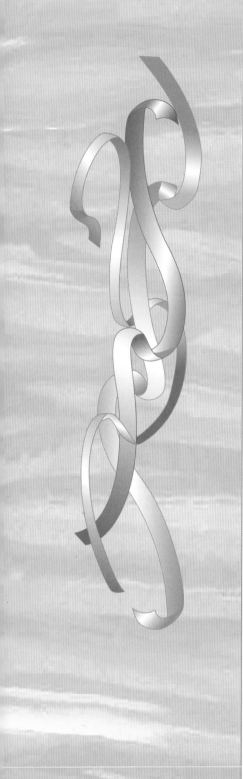

Topstitching Thread - a heavy weight thread requiring a larger, topstitching or denim needle in the machine. It is perfect for sewing in background elements. Cordonnet thread by Mettler is a good choice with a large color range.

Rayon Embroidery Thread - used as single strand and paired with your machine's floral decorative stitches, creates beautiful effects. A double or triple strand of rayon thread can be sewn into beefy vines using a slightly longer, simple straight stitch.

Beads and Pearls

The more embroidery I sew, the more visual activity I like to see in a piece. Adding small beads and pearls is an effective way to texturize and add excitement to your work.

BEADS

Choose glass beads to hold up during both washing and dry cleaning, buying the best you can afford. When purchasing beads to sew on by machine, make sure that the center hole is large enough to accommodate a #60 or #70 sewing machine needle. To test, take a needle with you when shopping. Insert the needle into the bead before buying.

PEARLS

The most easily found pearls are the craft variety which have a plastic pearlized coating over a small plastic ball core. This coating may peel or come loose during repeated washing and drying cycles. This is not critical on non-garment projects, such as needlework canvases, photo frames, albums or small accessories. Seek out a reputable bead source for higher quality pearls if placing on garments.

THE NECESSARY SUPPLIES

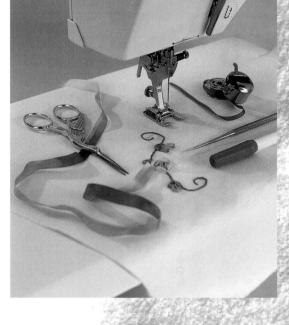

When beginning any sewing project, nothing saves time like having all the right tools assembled and ready to use. Take a moment to organize a silk ribbon "toolbox", including marking pens, embroidery scissors, stiletto, and so on, all ready to use when you begin.

Included on the following pages is a "soup to nuts" listing of the products used to create all the projects in this book. You'll be surprised, many of them are already in your sewing room!

Sewing Machine

A good quality, well cleaned and oiled sewing machine in good working order is critical to any sewing project. Basic straight and zig-zag stitches, plus the ability to raise and lower your feed dogs, are basic features to reproduce almost all silk ribbon machine work.

Additional features that I find indispensable are:

Needle Down - a function that automatically lowers the needle into the fabric at the end of stitching.

Pattern Extend/Double - a function that doubles, triples or extends even more some programmed stitches without losing their shape—terrific for silk ribbon bobbinwork.

Pattern Begin - automatically sets the machine to restart at the beginning of a motif. It's a lifesaver for flawless embroidery bridging after running out of thread or ribbon.

TIP: If your feed dogs can't be lowered easily, cover them with a piece of masking tape to counteract the feeding motion. Due to the friction caused by fabric movement, the tape may need to be replaced during the project.

Sewing Machine Needles

Since the silk ribbon never passes through the eye of the needle, needle size is matched in size and type to the fabrics used. Universal needles/Sharps are suggested for wovens. Ballpoint needles are recommended for knits. Embroidery needles work best for background embroidery, using built-in, pre-programmed motifs from your machine.

Specialty Presser Feet

Open Embroidery Foot - When stitching background vines, embroidered motifs or bobbinwork, the visibility afforded by a foot with a totally cut front is invaluable. This foot also works particularly well when stitching criss-cross chainstitch vines with topstitching thread or narrow ribbons.

Darning Foot - Because this foot is spring loaded and stops slightly above the surface of the fabric, fabric maneuverability is at an optimum. Free motion, fill-in embroidery is smoothly sewn. See Chapter 7, Mixed Media and Chapter 9, "Sunflower Garden" vest.

Open Darning Foot - Similar to the darning foot, this free motion foot has a cut out front, allowing better visibility when stitching free motion applications.

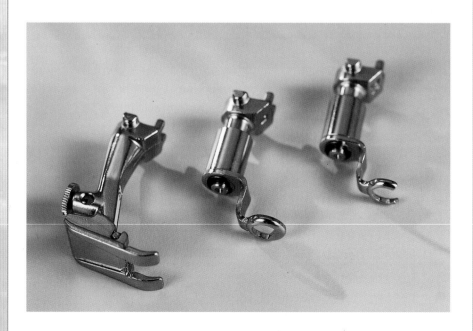

Secondary Bobbin Cases

Bobbinwork techniques involve loosening the tension set screw on your bobbin case. It is highly recommended that you purchase a second bobbin case especially for this purpose. Check with your local sewing machine dealer for the correct bobbin case for these techniques. Sometimes, a case with a pre-blackened latch will be available. For other machines, a duplicate of your standard case will work just fine. Permanently mark this bobbin case by placing a dot of nail polish on the latch so you don't confuse it with your standard case.

Marking Tools

I've had the most creative fun freehand drawing designs directly onto the garments and projects in the book. Each different fabric, color, and fiber content required different marking tools. The products listed below work well for me. As with all markers, test in an inconspicuous section of your project to be assured the marks will come out.

Water Soluble, Fade-Away Marking Pens - Soft or hard tipped, these purple inked marking pens mark successfully on a variety of light to medium-colored fabrics. The ink fades away within 24 to 48 hours (faster on a rainy day!) or can be immediately removed with cold water.

Quilter's Silver Lead Marking Pencil - This silver lead pencil favored by quilters gives a sharp, thin line for marking designs. The thinness of the marking is easily covered by subsequent embroidery.

Soapstone Marker - Ideal for marking on dark fabrics, this tool consists of a pen-like metal barrel that holds a full length solid soapstone tube. Sharpened with a pencil sharpener, the lines created with this marker can be removed with water without leaving any residue.

White Ink Marking Pen - A fine point (1.0 mm) white ink marking pen is needed for transferring designs to wash-away stabilizer film needed for embellishing napped fabrics, such as velvet and velveteen. The medium soft point is hard enough to produce an easily followed line, yet will not tear the wash-out stabilizer film. The Sakura Pen-Touch™ white, fine point, 1.0mm marker has a quick-dry ink and it dependably marks every time.

Tracing Products

When it is necessary for a design to be traced exactly, there are many methods which will work. See Chapter 4, The Beginning and Care of Each Project for details. The products that were tested for exact transferring are:

Tracing Paper - the Saral brand Wax Free Transfer Paper produces smudgeless transfers.

Wash-away Stabilizer - working with a white ink marking pen, designs can be traced onto this wash-away stabilizer film and removed with water after embroidery is complete.

Bridal Tulle - designs are traced on a single layer of tulle and placed onto the embroidery project. After embroidery, the tulle is clipped away.

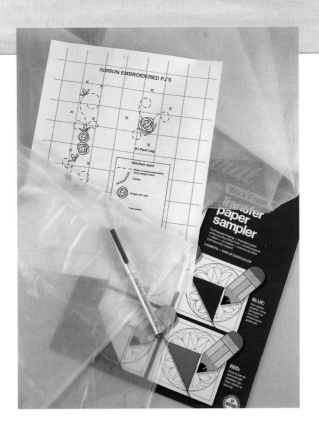

Scissors

Good quality, sharp scissors are a must for any sewing project. Besides a fine pair of dressmaker shears, consider these specialty scissors:

Embroidery Scissors - Usually available in 4" - 6" lengths, these small sized scissors are designed with long sharp tips, ideal for snipping threads and ribbons in hard to reach places.

Appliqué Scissors - The long sharp tips of these scissors also make them good for snipping. However, the duckbill blade is indispensable when sewing the reverse appliqué technique featured in Chapter 9, "Confetti Scraps" vest.

Stiletto

A long handled, sharp pointed stiletto tool is handy for safely holding down ribbons during couching techniques This pencil-like metal

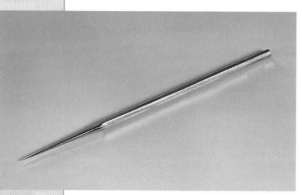

stick replaces pins and fingers, allowing the sewer to stitch right next to the point, fine tuning ribbon placement when tacking.

Embroidery Hoops

Keeping your work as taut as possible while embroidering prevents puckers in the final product. Place your embroidery area in a hoop whenever possible. Select high-quality, hardwood embroidery hoops for strength. Low profile hoops allow the sewer to insert and remove the hoop from the bed of the machine without having to take of the presser foot.

For an even tighter fit, wrap the inner ring of your embroidery hoop with twill tape before using.

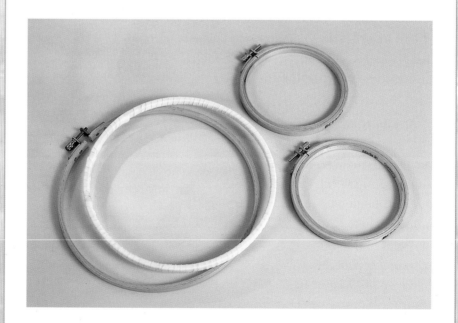

Specialty Hand Sewing Needles

Ribbon tails need to be drawn to the wrong side of your project and secured. These special needles are recommended:

Tapestry Needles - Large-eyed and blunt-tipped, ribbon is easily threaded onto these needles. Due to the blunt tip, they work best on knits.

Silk Ribbon Embroidery Needles - Akin to chenille needles, these sharp pointed, wide-eyed needles are usually packed in multiple sizes for handwork enthusiasts. They are especially good on wovens and needlework canvases, piercing the fibers easily.

Pin-weaving Press Board

A gridded, pinnable pressing surface is wonderful when weaving your own silk ribbon yardage. The June Tailor, Pin-Weave Express™, features a horizontal and vertical grid, marked off in ½" increments, generously sized for weaving yardage small or large.

Chapter Four

THE BEGINNING AND CARE OF EACH PROJECT

Once you've selected your design, garment or fabric to embellish, it's time to get to work. Careful fabric preparation and finishing details are as important as the embroidery in between. Stabilizing the embroidery area, transferring designs, as well as final care "post embroidery," are discussed in this chapter.

 TIP: If stabilizing a purchased garment, lift any facing pieces away from the area to be pressed. An unsightly ridge line caused by catching the facing while fusing will be eliminated.

Pre-Embroidery Steps

1. Stabilize the area to be embroidered. Whether it's a garment, accessory or needlework canvas, you will be adding additional weight and stress to the fabric with silk ribbons and additional embroidery. These areas need to be supported. Fuse them with a lightweight woven or knit interfacing. I find a fusible tricot interfacing, such as Easy Knit™ or Sof Shapes™, adds integrity to the work without stiffness. Pink the edges of the interfacing piece prior to fusing to soften the edges.

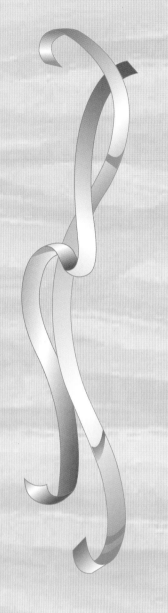

Fuse stabilizers with these products:

High-quality Iron - A heavy, high-quality iron with a non-stick sole plate is ideal for first time success in fusing interfacings. Follow the manufacturers suggested times and methods for fusing for the best results.

Tabletop Press - Fusing time is cut in half with a large ironing surface, increased steam output and heavyweight lids. A full vest front can be completely fused in a matter of seconds. State-of-the-art models include built-in timers and computer programming capabilities for pressing.

2. Trace the desired design using one of these methods:

Tracing Paper - Trace the desired design onto a sheet of plain white paper. Use a light box or hold the design onto a window for best visibility. Place the traced design onto the garment with a sheet of tracing paper in between the design and fabric. Using a pen, transfer the traced design onto the fabric, while pressing down on the paper.

White Ink/Water-Soluble Stabilizer Method - Use this method for transferring designs onto fabrics that cannot be drawn upon. Trace the design onto a sheet of water-soluble stabilizer using a white ink marker. Cut away the excess stabilizer and pin the traced design onto the right side of the embroidery area. Stitch the ribbon design directly through the stabilizer. Remove the excess film by cutting away larger pieces. Release any excess film by touching the film with moistened cotton to dissolve.

Tulle Method - Place a single layer of bridal tulle over the desired design. Using a fade-away marker or fine tipped marking pen, trace over the design, transferring it onto the tulle. Pin the tulle to the project's right side. Stitch through the tulle, clipping away excess tulle when complete.

TIP: Place the project on a hard surface for best tracing results.

3. As you place your project in a hoop ready for embroidery, it's important to remember to keep the fabric as close to the feed dogs as possible. Therefore, the large part of the hoop is placed down first, then your fabric placed over it, followed by the smaller, inner ring. Loosen the hoop's tension screw prior to hooping, tightening the screw once the fabric is in position.
4. Support the embroidery stitches with tear-away stabilizer when sewing in the background. The stabilizer is placed underneath the hoop and on top of the feed dogs.

Now that your work is stabilized in a hoop and ready to stitch, take a deep breath and let the creativity begin.

Finishing Your Silk Ribbon Project

After all the ribbon embroidery is complete, follow these final finishing and care steps:

1. Secure all loose threads and ribbon tails. Draw all loose ends to the project's wrong side and knot off. Fuse down tails or weave the ribbon ends in between bobbin stitches or fabric fibers.
2. Press carefully. Adjust your steam iron for a setting appropriate to the base fabric. Press carefully all around the silk ribbon embellishment. If needed, press your embroidery in one of two ways: Hold the steam iron a few inches above the embroidery right sides up. Allow the steam to only smooth out the ribbons.

Or with right side down, lay your embroidery on a velvet needleboard or an extra fluffy bath towel. June Tailor's Velvaboard™ has a soft, pressable surface that will allow light pressing without crushing any embroidery motifs.

 TIP: Load an extra fine mist spray bottle with cold water. Mist the crushed and wilted flower embroidery. Your flowers will "bloom" again and become dimensional. This tip was offered by silk ribbon dye artists.

Dry Clean or Wash?

The manufacturers and dye studios interviewed for this book agreed that their products can be both dry cleaned and washed. Dry cleaning the project was suggested as the safest option with the most reliable results.

However, for those of you who prefer washing, everyone interviewed recommended a cold water wash and line drying of your projects. Choose a gentle soap, such as Dreft™ or Ivory Snow™, to retain the beauty of the silk ribbon colorations. We were advised that stronger laundry products often have ingredients that can fade and dull the brilliance of the ribbons.

 Cover the nozzle of a vacuum cleaner hose with two layers of tulle creating a gentler suction in the hose during the cleaning process. Vacuum a few inches away from the canvas. The tulle will allow the dust to pass through, but catch any loose ribbons or beads. This tip was offered by museum curators of costume collections for cleaning vintage garments.

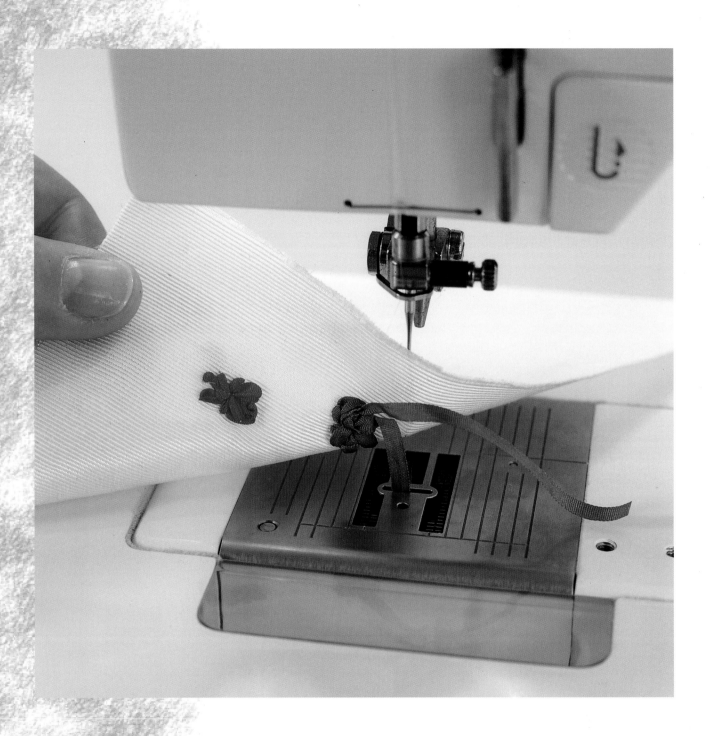

Chapter Five

SILK RIBBON BOBBINWORK

Many built-in sewing machine stitches take on a new elegance when silk ribbon is used in the bobbin and sewn using a technique called bobbinwork. Humble straight stitches become vines, utility and motif stitches blossom into a garden full of flowers.

Bobbinwork Defined

Technically, bobbinwork is simply described as upside-down sewing. Heavy decorative threads or ribbons too thick to pass through the eye of a needle are wound onto a bobbin and inserted into a secondary bobbin case with a loosened tension. All-purpose thread, color-matched to the ribbon and project or monofilament thread is used in the needle. To accommodate the width of the ribbon, stitch lengths are usually lengthened or pattern sizes doubled. For sewing machine models that do not have a removable bobbin case, manufacturers suggest bypassing the tension hook or threading the ribbon directly through an opening on the machine's throat plate. Check with your local dealer or sewing machine guidebook for the method best suited to your individual machine.

Designs to be embroidered are marked and sewn on the wrong side of

the fabric, adding a touch of suspense and drama when turning over your work to see the results! Ribbon tails are hand-sewn to the wrong side using a large-eyed tapestry needle and secured with the needle thread tails.

Silk Ribbon Sizes and Types

The best, jam-free results are achieved on the sewing machine using 2 - 4mm wide silk ribbons. Due to their width, 7mm wide ribbons respond with limited success, feeding unevenly or jamming. The silk and man-made silk look-alikes tested and sewn successfully on the machine are listed here by brand name:

▌ Silk Ribbon™ by YLI Corporation (100% silk)

▌ Heirloom Sylk™ by Mokuba (100% Azlon)

▌ Pure Silk Ribbon by Bucilla (100% silk)

▌ Petals™ hand-dyed silk ribbon by Sweet Child of Mine (100% silk)

▌ Elegance Ribbons™ by Island Fibers (100% silk)

Ribbon Loading and Bobbin case Tension

Handwind the ribbon onto an empty bobbin, keeping it as flat and taut as possible. To keep the ribbon from slipping when starting, thread the ribbon tail through one of the bobbins holes or slits. Wind the ribbon a few turns to secure, then clip the loose tail from the outside.

Continue to handwind in a smooth, even fashion. Unevenly wound bobbins can result in irregular stitches or feeding problems. Finish winding until the bobbin is almost full without the ribbon extending past the outer edges.

 TIP: To save time and aggravation when you are in the middle of a project, handwind a number of the same color bobbins at the beginning of your project before stitching.

Insert the filled bobbin into an alternate bobbin case. Loosen the tension set screw so the ribbon pulls freely with little tension. Place into your sewing machine as normal.

Needles and Threads

Match your needle size to the thread and fabrics used. A good quality cotton-wrapped polyester or 100% cotton thread, color matched to the silk ribbons, may be selected for the needle. Monofilament thread may also be used, but can require some additional tension adjustments due to the stretch of the thread.

Fabric Preparation

Always interface your fashion fabric before stitching since a great number of stitches will be sewn in a small area. A soft, pliable interfacing, such as a fusible tricot, adds body to the fabric without over stiffening it. If puckering occurs on a test sample, you may want to add an additional layer of interfacing. Select an interfacing in a white or ivory color because you will have better visibility while marking and sewing from the wrong side.

Stitch a Sampler

It's well worth your time to prepare your fabric and sew a sampler of your machine's stitches with silk ribbon. Multiple sampler squares showing simple utility and decorative patterns sewn in 2mm and 4mm ribbons can be combined in a notebook to create your personal stitch library for future projects.

Cut a 12" square of solid fabric and back it with a square of the appropriate weight interfacing. Lightweight fusible tricot provides just enough body and stability without adding stiffness to a project. Draw lines 1" apart from left to right on the interfacing side. Select a stitch, beginning with a normal length and width. With the interfacing side up, sew for 3" following the first line, stopping the needle in the down position to hold your place. Draw an intersecting line across your path of sewing and, with a pen, mark the upper tension setting and stitch length and width at which you began. Increase the stitch length by ½ to 1 full number.

TIP: Since you are loosening the tension set screw on the bobbin case, use a separate bobbin case when sewing with bulky threads. By doing this, you won't have to spend time later trying to figure out the best, balanced tension for normal sewing.

Loosen the upper tension, if desired. Sew another 3", stopping again to note the width, length and tension settings. Continue sewing and marking until the sampler is full or the desired stitches have been tested.

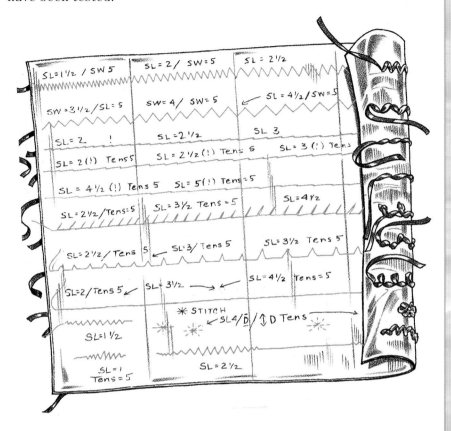

Basic built-in utility stitches through open-designed decorative patterns can be sewn successfully using the bobbinwork technique. Remember to adjust each stitch for longer than usual lengths. Take advantage of your machine's computerized capabilities, such as, doubling the size of a pattern or engaging a Long Stitch function which will makes the machine sew every other stitch of the pattern.

Listed below are a few stitch recommendations to get you started. Select open, airy stitch patterns that have a lot of space between individual stitches to allow for the bulk of the silk ribbon. Some satin stitch patterns can be used, but need to be lengthened to avoid excess ribbon build-up.

Many more potential ribbon designs are available to you through your own machine's design package. Experiment and have fun! While testing, be aware that the stitch length and tension recommendations given above are just that—recommendations, and may need to be adjusted based upon your own machine's personality.

STITCH CHOICE	RECOMMENDED LENGTH	RECOMMENDED WIDTH	UPPER TENSION	ADDITIONAL COMMENTS
Straight Stitch	4-4¼mm		Normal-slightly loose	Engage Long Stitch (if available)
Zig-Zag Stitch	1½-4mm	5-10mm	Nomal-slightly tight	Tighten needle tension to create fullest width with no needle show through
Jersey Stitch	1½-4mm	5-9mm	Normal	
Blanket Stitch	4½-5mm	5-9mm	Normal	
Star of Daisy Stitch	Double Pattern Size	5-9mm	Normal	Engage Long Stitch (if available). Sew single pattern.
Cross Stitch	Double or Triple Size	Machine Preset	Normal	

Free-motion Embroidery

Another method of creating beautiful designs with bobbinwork is working in free-motion. Like the free-motion embroidery technique, the feed dogs are lowered and you are guiding the fabric under the needle since there is no feeding motion of the fabric. Make a sampler of various sized roses and daisies utilizing this technique.

The machine set-up for free-motion bobbinwork is similar to that of built-in stitches. Select an all-purpose polyester thread for the needle that is color-coordinated to the ribbon and the project. Wind a number of bobbins with the appropriate colored silk ribbon. Adjust the bobbin case tension as before. The upper tension should be set at the normal setting or slightly loosened. Lower or disengage the feed dogs on your machine and you are ready to go. If you have a Needle Down function on your machine, it is helpful if the needle always stops down with this technique.

Roses

Beginning in the center of your interfaced sampler fabric, sew in a tiny circle, gently increasing the spiral on each rotation. After the desired size has been stitched, peek to the right side of the fabric to see if the rose appears filled in. Stitch around a second time to fill in any blank areas if necessary. Once all the roses are complete, using a large-eyed tapestry needle, draw the ribbon and thread tails to the wrong side. Knot the ribbon with the needle thread. Clip, leaving a ½" tail.

Zig-Zag Daisies

For this technique, adjust the stitch width to 5 - 9mm depending on your machine. The upper tension is tightened to 8 –10. Lower the feed dogs and follow the normal procedures for silk ribbon bobbinwork.

On your sampler mark two short intersecting lines where the first daisy is desired. Insert your needle in the center, at the intersection of the lines. Stitch two right to left sets of zig-zags, ending in the center. With the needle in the fabric, pivot to sew the second petal in the opposite direction. Sew two more sets of zig-zags, again ending in the center. With the needle in the fabric, pivot the fabric to the adjacent drawn unsewn line, sew two sets of right/left zig-zags, ending at center. Pivot and complete the fourth petal. Sew four more sets of petals in between the first four sewn to complete flower. Draw ribbon tails to the wrong side of the fabric using a large-eyed tapestry needle. Knot the ribbon tails with the needle thread tails to secure. Clip.

A combination of built-in stitches and free-motion bobbinwork allows you to design with endless possibilities. Try your skills on the following projects which highlight both silk ribbon bobbinwork techniques.

RIBBON EMBELLISHED PHOTO ALBUM

Skill Level: Beginner

TECHNIQUE HIGHLIGHTED:
Sewing simple built-in patterns with bobbinwork.

Transform a simple, plain photo album into a cherished family heirloom with uncomplicated machine stitches, elegant fabrics and silk ribbon bobbinwork!

Materials:

- Purchased photo album
- Fabric(such as moiré, satin, velveteen)—yardage based on size of album
- Fusible tricot interfacing—same as photo album cover fabric
- Rectangle of polyester fleece or batting—front, back, and spine measurement
- Fade-way fabric marker or tailor's chalk
- Braid trim to cover inside front and back covers at edges
- Assorted colors of 4mm silk ribbons
- Tacky glue
- Optional: 1 yd. of 1½" wide satin ribbon for ties

Directions:

1. Place the decorative fabric on a work surface with the wrong side up. Lay the opened photo album onto the fabric and trace around the outer edge with a fabric marker or chalk. Remove the album from the fabric and add 2" to the outside of all traced edges. Cut the decorative fabric along the outer lines.

2. Cut and fuse a piece of tricot interfacing to the full size of the album cover piece.

3. Baste along the inner traced lines marking the exact size of the photo album. If the lines are faint, retrace them directly onto the fused interfacing. This basting line will provide you with a permanent guideline against which to gauge your embroidery lengths.

 TIP: You may also want to mark and baste placement lines on the fused rectangle for the album spine to help in planning the overall embroidery designs.

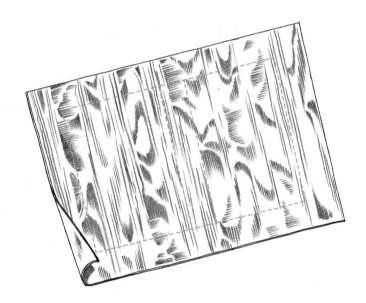

4. Cut a piece of polyester fleece the size of the inner basted line.

5. Set up the sewing machine for the bobbinwork embroidery stitches of your choice. Load a ribbon-wound bobbin into the loosened bobbin case. Thread the needle with a color-coordinated thread.

6. Mark embroidery design lines with a fabric or chalk marker on the fusible knit interfacing. The diagram listed in the back of the book shows stitch selections and placement for the sample photographed.

TIP; Fuse your ribbon tails to the wrong side to secure instead of knotting them. After sewing three or four rows of stitches, use a large-eyed tapestry needle to bring the ribbon tails to the wrong side. Press ½" squares of fusible interfacing over the ribbon and bobbin thread tails, securing the tails without bulk.

7. When all the embroidery is complete, prepare the album for the outer cover. Glue the polyester fleece to the outside of the album.

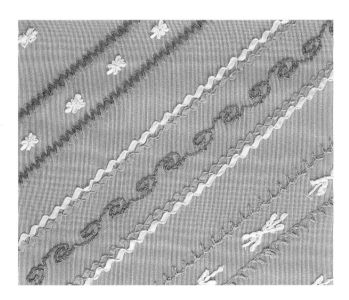

8. Center and glue the embroidered fabric on top of the fleece, using the basting lines as guides. Wrap the excess fabric to the inside of the album, mitering the corners before gluing the edges down. Allow the album to fully dry.

9. Cut pieces of decorative fabric large enough to cover the inside of the front and back album cover and the wrapped edges. Glue decorative trim over any raw edges of the fabric to finish.

TIP: Satin ribbon ties can be glued between the front and back cover pieces if desired.

41

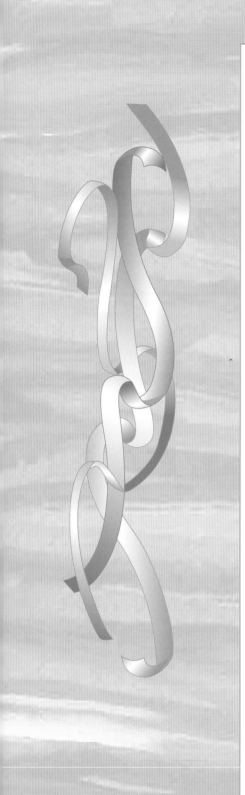

ELEGANT SACHET BAG

Skill Level: Advanced Beginner

**Techniques highlighted: Bobbinwork with built in stitches
Free-motion bobbinwork**

Combine free-motion and built-in stitch embroidery to create this delicate sachet bag to grace your favorite bureau drawer.

Materials:

- 12" x 9" piece of moiré or satin
- 12" x 9" piece lace
- Assorted colors of 2mm and 4mm silk ribbons
- 1½ yds of ⅜" wide satin ribbon
- 6" heavy lace edging
- 6" x 9" piece of fusible interfacing

Directions:

1. Cut two 6" x 9" pieces of decorative fabric for the sachet bag and two 6" x 9" pieces of the lace yardage.

2. Using the embroidery pattern given in the back of the book, trace the design onto the smooth side of the fusible interfacing. Fuse the interfacing to the wrong side of one of the 6" x 9" fabric pieces.

3. Refer to the design diagram on page 118 for stitch suggestions. Embroider all of the built-in stitch designs, first, using the bobbinwork machine set-up described earlier.

4. Additional free-motion bobbinwork is applied next. Follow the diagram in the back of the book for placement of the free-motion roses.

5. When the embroidery is finished, complete the bag. Lay one lace piece over the embroidered design. Draw and baste a window framing the embroidered area. Trim away the lace over the embroidery.

6. Set your machine for regular embroidery stitching, replace the bobbin with embroidery thread and load the standard bobbin case. Select a satin or decorative edging stitch and sew around the opening using the basting line as a guide.

7. Baste the lace overlay to all four outer edges of the bag front. Repeat on the bag back. Serge or clean finish all edges of the front and back pieces.

9. With right sides together, sew the bag along two sides and along the lower edge, leaving an opening for the ribbon casing.

10. Turn the bag right side out and press.

11. Turn down a 1" hem and stitch close to the edge to form a casing.

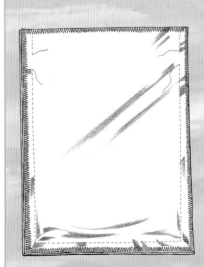

12. To create a double draw ribbon closure, cut the satin ribbon length in half. Insert one piece of ribbon into the opening on the right side of the bag, bypassing the left opening and exiting back at the right side opening. Repeat the same procedure with the second piece of ribbon, beginning and ending on the left. To close, pull both the left and right ribbons.

13. Fill the sachet bag with potpourri. Place your embroidered treasure in your favorite bureau drawer or give as a wonderful, special gift.

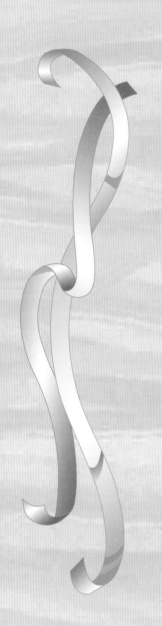

EMBROIDERED OVALS

Skill Level: Advanced Beginner

**Techniques Highlighted: Zig-Zag Stitch
Free Motion Bobbinwork**

Machine stitch basics are machine embroidered onto graceful ovals to become elegant jewelry or hair accents. The denim barrette sports a field full of flowers duplicating the popular Lazy Daisy stitch enjoyed by handwork enthusiasts. The velvet oval relies on machine feather and motif stitches as well as free-motion embroidered roses to create a textured floral spray.

Materials: (For one oval)

- 6" x 9" piece of fabric
- 6" x 6" piece of fusible tricot interfacing
- 4" x 4" square of polyester fleece
- 12" of braid trim
- 2¾" spring barrette or pin back
- 6" x 6" piece of heavy cardboard
- Tacky glue
- Optional: 3mm round or oval seed pearls

Directions:

1. From the decorative fabric, cut one piece, 6" x 6" square for embroidering. The remaining 6" x 3" piece will be used for the pin or barrette back.
2. Fuse the interfacing to the wrong side of the 6" x 6" piece of decorative fabric.
3. Using the template in the back of the book, center and trace the oval shape onto the back of the interfacing. Machine baste along this line. This basting line outlines the area inside which you will place your stitches.
4. Center and trace the embroidery designs found in the back of the book onto the fusible interfacing.

5. Embroider the floral designs onto the decorative fabric. Follow the diagram for placement and the instructions at the beginning of the chapter for built-in and free-motion flower silk ribbon bobbinwork techniques.

6. Using the oval template in the back of the book, cut one piece from heavy cardboard.

7. Glue a piece of polyester fleece to the oval, cutting the edges evenly.

9. Center and glue the embroidered fabric to the padded cardboard. Allow the piece to dry completely.

10. Trim away any excess fabric to within 1" of the cardboard edge. Pull the basting stitches to gather the edge of the fabric evenly around the oval. Glue the edges in place on the back of the cardboard.

11. Cut an oval for the back from the 3" x 6" scrap. Glue this piece to the cardboard, covering the raw edges of the fabric.

12. Glue a decorative trim to the back of the oval covering any raw edges and allowing the picot edge to extend slightly past the outer edge. Hot glue or hand sew a pin backing or barrette clip to the back of the oval.

Chapter Six

SILK RIBBONS COUCHED FROM THE TOP

The dimensional beauty of handworked silk ribbon embroidery can easily be duplicated on the sewing machine by couching or tacking the ribbons in place. With practice, and careful study of how the individual flowers are formed, sewing machine enthusiasts can duplicate most patterns designed for hand stitching.

A Definition

Traditional sewing machine couching refers to tacking or zig-zag sewing heavy cords, trims or ribbons down on the right side of your fabric. Silk ribbon couching is created this way. Ribbons are anchored at the start of a design. The ribbon is moved out of the way as you sew to the next ribbon anchor point. The ribbon is tacked down, and moved again while sewing to the next position. The flower or bud is completed this way. Ribbon tails are tucked underneath a petal, machine sewn into place and clipped. They may also be hand-sewn to the fabric's wrong side and tied or fused down to secure. For invisible stitches, use monofilament thread in the needle, and all-purpose thread in the bobbin, color matched to your fashion fabric. Since the wide ribbon does not pass through the eye of the needle, select a needle size appropriate to your fabric. Designs can be sewn on flat fabrics or ready-to-wear garments. A hoop may or may not be used, depending upon the fabrics used and embroidery location on the ready-to-wear garment.

You will get the most mileage from your silk ribbon yardage using this technique, as bits and pieces of silk can be effectively tucked and manipulated into small buds and leaves.

47

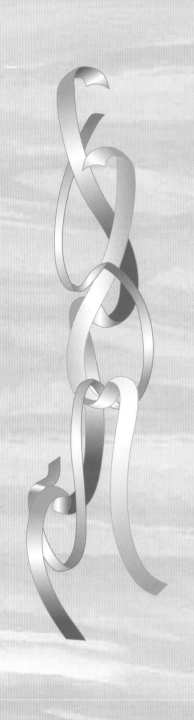

General Supplies for Silk Ribbon Couching:
- Sewing machine in good working order
- Needles appropriately sized to fashion fabric
- Fine monofilament thread, like YLI's Wonder™ thread
- Good quality all-purpose polyester for bobbin
- Open toe or clear plastic embroidery foot
- Wooden machine embroidery hoop
- Small embroidery scissors
- Long handled serger tweezers, stiletto or large needle
- Fade-away fabric marker
- Heat transfer pens
- White marking pen
- Water soluble stabilizer, such as Solvy™
- Assorted silk ribbons in a variety of sizes
- Topstitching thread and topstitch needles for vine sewing options

Creating and Duplicating Patterns for Silk Ribbon Couching

Designs offered in this book, other silk ribbon embroidery books or original works of art can be transferred for embroidery in a number of ways. Depending upon the fashion fabric chosen, color and pile, one of the following methods should work for you.

HEAT TRANSFER PEN METHOD

Appropriate for transferring designs onto light to medium colored, flat finish fabrics, these pens by Sulky of America are available in five colors, and yield multiple transfers with just one inking. Follow the manufacturer's directions on the packaging to create transfer pages most like those found in silk ribbon embroidery pattern booklets.

WHITE MARKING PEN/WATER-SOLUBLE STABILIZER METHOD

When working on dark colored and heavy napped fabrics, such as velvet and velveteens, try this method for design transfer. Trace your design onto a single layer piece of water-soluble stabilizer, such as Solvy™, by Sulky of America. Pin the stabilizer in place on the right side of your fashion fabric. Stitch the silk ribbon design through the traced stabilizer.

Carefully pull away the stabilizer from the machine stitches, using a moistened cotton swab to dab away any whiskers of stabilizer left over.

FADE-AWAY MARKER OR CHALK TRACINGS

Original designs can simply be drawn right onto your fashion fabric using an air-soluble fabric marker or dressmakers chalk. Remember, though, to stitch quickly when using the markers, as they can fade in 24 - 48 hours.

Beginning Your Design

SEWING VINES

Most hand-worked silk ribbon designs feature a background of trailing embroidered vines laid down before adding silk ribbon flowers. Creating consistent, even, hand-worked stitches can be quite a challenge. Luckily, most all sewing machines have some sort of simple, straight stitch that can effortlessly duplicate a hand-sewn stab or running stitch.

Select a #100 needle. and Cordonnet or topstitching thread, or 2–3 strands of all-purpose polyester, rayon or cotton embroidery

TIP: When using 2-3 strands of the same thread, wind additional bobbins from the original spool. Place them on the spool pin in opposite directions. If needed, lengthen the spool pin with a drinking straw to accommodate the bobbins.

threaded through one needle. Use all-purpose thread color matched to the fashion fabric in the bobbin. An open toe or clear embroidery foot will provide the best visibility.

Using a fade-away fabric marker, draw in some trailing vines. Precision isn't necessary. Have fun and design what looks good to your eye. Place your garment in the embroidery hoop, adjusting the tension set screw for the tightest fit. If possible, push the lower portion of the hoop $\frac{1}{8}$" lower than the upper ring to build in extra tautness. Place your hooped design under the presser foot of your sewing machine. With your machine set on an average length, normal straight stitch, take one stitch. Pull up on the needle thread to bring the bobbin thread to the top. Sew forwards and backwards over all the thread tails two to three times to secure. Clip the loose ends close to your work. Reset your machine to stitch in the vines using any of the following stitches:

Straight stitch - (SL: 4-5) Use buttonhole twist or two to three strands of rayon or cotton embroidery thread. This is a good stitch for control in curved vine areas.

Triple-Straight Stitch - (SL: 4-5) Use a single strand of all-purpose, rayon or cotton embroidery thread. This commonly found stitch sews forwards and backwards over itself, building up thread density in the same spot. Do not use this stitch with heavier topstitching threads. It is the best stitch for long, somewhat straight vines due to the overstitching motion.

Feather Stitch - (SL 4-5) All threads will work well with this stitch. Sewn with a straight stitch and a diagonal, this stitch pattern adds an extra design element to a vine.

BUDS AND LEAVES

After clipping your secured vine tails, plan the positioning of your buds and leaves. Both are created using the same simple loop stitch. Remember how nature creates flowers—leaves encase the buds. Therefore, sew the bud first, then leaves to the left and right.

Set your machine with a needle sized according to the fashion fabric and threaded with monofilament thread. Place all-purpose thread color matched to fashion fabric in the bobbin. Attach an open or clear embroidery foot. Adjust the SL to 1½ – 2mm.

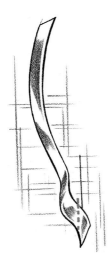

To create buds, use a fade away fabric marker and draw one straight line the length desired for the flower bud. Tack a piece of silk ribbon at the bud base, securing with two to three stitches.

Move the ribbon out of the way. Straight stitch to the top of the drawn line. Stop with the needle in the down position. Swing the ribbon up to the needle, holding in place with long tweezers. Tack with two machine stitches.

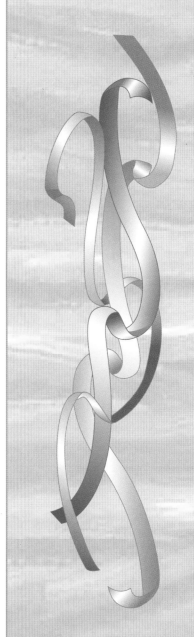

TIP: Vary the look of your buds and leaves by, pinching the ribbon as it is being tacked down to add dimension. Twist the ribbon slightly before tacking or use two colors of a narrower sized ribbon to create a two-toned effect.

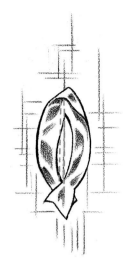

Pivot 180˚, sew down to the starting point. Swing the ribbon to the lowered needle, tack in place at the base of the bud. Remove from the sewing machine and clip ribbon close to stitching.

For leaves. draw two lines to the left and right of the sewn ribbon bud.

Repeat steps 2–5 from the bud directions to create leaves.

Optional Leaf Finish: If the cut edges of the ribbon at the leaf base are not desired, leave a 4" tail of ribbon after tacking the last stitch. Thread the ribbon through a large eye embroidery needle and hand sew the tail to the wrong side. Knot with bobbin thread or fuse in place.

For the easiest machine stitching, drop your feed dogs and sew these flowers free-motion. Placing your fabric in a hoop, whenever possible, will help guide stitching, however, some fabrics, such as velvets will be damaged by being in a hoop. Also, areas to be embroidered on ready-made garments may not fit into a hoop easily. Embroidering without a hoop in these cases is recommended and your design can be sewn successfully.

FLOWERS

Once the vines, leaves and buds are sewn down, have fun creating spectacular ribbon flowers. Some designs that follow duplicate traditional hand-work patterns, while others are fantasy flowers just for fun. You'll find inspiration blooming from your sewing machine the longer you work with the ribbons. The possibilities are endless. Here are a few designs to get you started:

Couched Lazy Daisy

First, draw a cross with both lines of an equal length. Tack 4mm silk ribbon at the flower center with 2-3 stitches. Keeping the ribbon away from the needle, stitch up to the top of the drawn line. Tack ribbon.

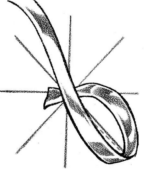

Pivot 180° and sew back to the starting point. Swing the ribbon around the needle, tacking to slightly overlap at the center.

Travel to the opposite and adjacent lines drawn for petals two, three and four, tacking and forming petals using the same technique. Stitch petals five through eight in between the first four petals sewn. Tack the final petal at center. Clip the ends and finish the center with a bead or French knot.

Small Looped Flowers

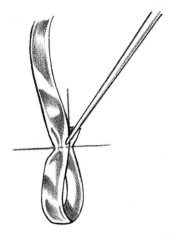

Using a fabric marker, draw a small cross on the fabric, lines of equal length. Tack ribbon at center with two to three stitches. Loop the ribbon up to the petal end and back to the center, keeping it as flat as possible. Tack at center.

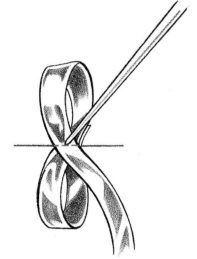

Repeat looping and tacking petals two through four, finishing at the center.

Clip ribbon and add a small bead or French knot at center.

Spider Flower

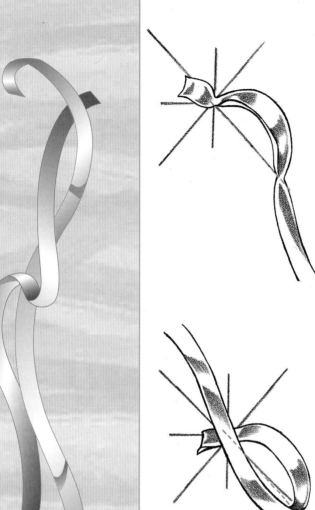

Draw an **uneven**, eight-petaled design similar to the Lazy Daisy. Anchor the ribbon at the center of the design as in Lazy Daisy. Stitch to the petal tip and tack, keeping the ribbon loose and slightly separated. Pivot 180° and sew back to the center.

Anchor the ribbon at the flower center and travel to the petal opposite the first.

Create the second petal in the same manner. Continue until all the petals are complete. Finish by securing ribbon at the flower center and embellish over the clipped end.

Knotted Spider Flower

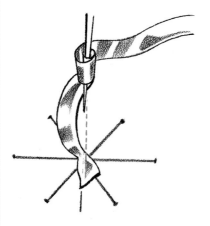

Draw a design the same as the standard Spider Flower. Begin the petals from the center as in spider flower. At the petal tip, tack the ribbon and lower the needle into the fabric. Wrap the ribbon around the needle two times and tack the knot at the petal top.

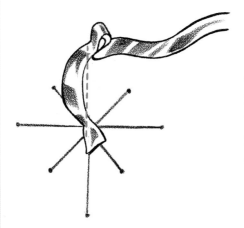

Sew back to the flower center, keeping the ribbon free. Bring the ribbon tail to the center and anchor in place. A tiny knot accent will appear on each petal tip.

Complete the remainder of petals using the knotted petal technique. Fill in the rest of the flower in the same manner as the spider flower.

Loopy Chrysanthemums

Draw a circle the approximate size desired for your flower. Anchor three strands of ribbon, halfway between the center and the outer edge of the drawn circle, cut ends towards the center, tails facing out.

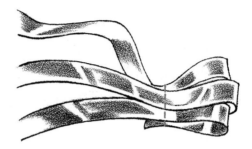

Using a stiletto or large needle, loop the ribbons towards the center and tack down. Pivot the fabric, flip the ribbons slightly downward and away from the center. Loop them again towards the center and sew down.

Repeat pivoting and loop tacking until the circle is filled and flower is complete.

Simple Coiled Rose

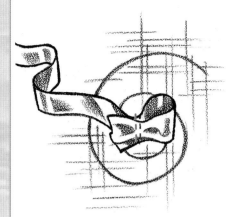

Draw a small spiral the size of the desired rose. Tack the ribbon in place at the center with two or three stitches.

TIP: For beautiful roses, 7mm ribbon gives spectacular results. Allow the ribbon to twist while sewing for added visual interest. "Crimp" the ribbon when tacking by inserting the point of the needle at the ribbon edge and pulling towards the center before sewing down. This will produce small, delicate gathers in each petal.

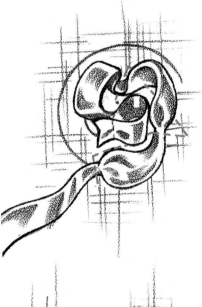

Following the drawn coil, position the ribbon ⅓ of the circle's diameter away from the center and anchor in place. Use long tweezers, stiletto or needle to hold ribbon in place. Keeping the ribbon free, sew to a second mark, approximately ⅔ around the drawn coil. Tack ribbon in place. Sew to a final third position to complete the first round of petals.

Repeat the pivoting and tacking procedure until the rose is generously full. Tuck the ribbon tail under a petal and secure in place with a few machine stitches.

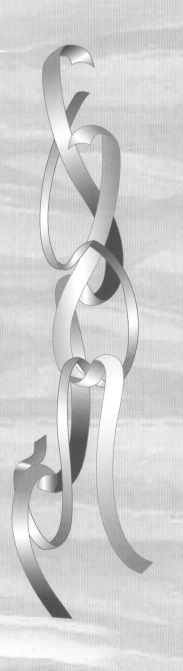

French Knots

Tack the ribbon down at the flower center.

Lower the needle into the fabric and wrap it with ribbon three to five times.

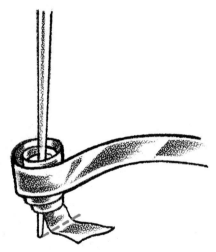

Carefully raise the needle and tack the coil in place.

Clip the ribbon, leaving a ¼" tail. Dot the tail with seam sealant and snip closer when dry.

Silk Ribbon Chainstitch - (SL 3-4) Place monofilament in the needle and all-purpose in the bobbin. Cut a piece of 2mm or 4mm ribbon, $2\frac{1}{2}$ to 3 times the finished length needed. Fold the ribbon in half and tack the mid-point of the ribbon down at the beginning of the vine. Sew two stitches, lower the needle into the fabric, raise the presser foot and criss cross the ribbons. Lower the presser foot, sew two more stitches, lower the needle, criss cross the ribbons, and lower the presser foot. Repeat until vine is stitched. Leave the thread tails long enough to thread to the fabric back using a large eye tapestry needle. Knot or fuse in place.

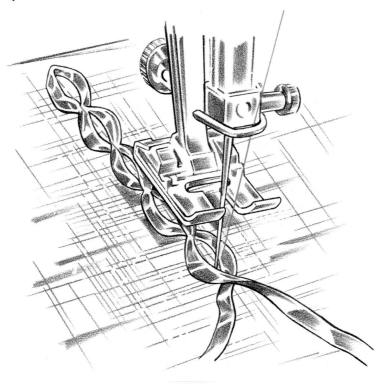

RIBBON EMBROIDERED PJs

Skill Level: Beginner

Techniques highlighted: Straight stitched vines; Silk ribbon couching - Buds and leaves; Simple Coiled Rose

You'll have sweet dreams wearing this elegantly embroidered bedtime ensemble with silk flower adornment.

Materials:

- Purchased silk pajama set
- Assorted 4mm and 7mm silk ribbons
- Heat transfer pen
- Monofilament thread
- All-purpose thread—color matched to fashion fabric
- Small wooden embroidery hoop
- Optional: 2mm pearls

Directions:

1. Using a heat transfer pen, trace the embroidery designs given in the back of the book onto paper. Following manufacturer's directions, transfer the designs to the desired garment location. If possible, place the areas to be embroidered in an embroidery hoop.
3. Following the individual stitch directions, embellish the garment in the following order:
   - Vines—sewn with desired vine stitch
   - Buds and Leaves— using 4 mm silk
   - Coiled Roses— using 7mm silk
   - Optional: add 2mm pearls as desired.

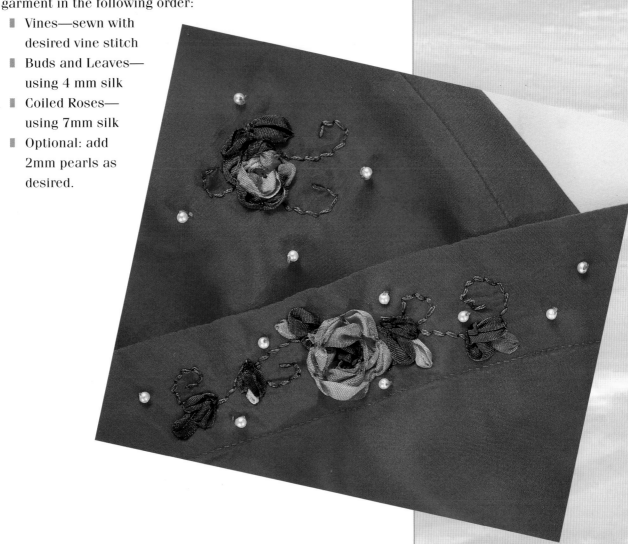

VELVET HANDBAG

Skill Level: Advanced Beginner

Techniques Highlighted: Chainstitch vine; Buds and Leaves; Loopy Chrysanthemums

Stitch an evening bag with turn of the century elegance and dramatic ribbon and beadwork.

Materials:

- ¼ yd each of velvet and lining fabrics
- Assorted 4mm and 7mm silk ribbons
- Monofilament thread
- All-purpose thread on bobbin—color matched to velvet
- Long tweezers, stiletto or large needle
- White ink transfer pen
- Water-soluble stabilizer
- ⅓ yd of 2" wide fringe
- From Ornamental Resources:
    Gold plated purse frame # 6081-FD
    12" gold plated purse chain #5654-FD

Directions:

1. Trace the design given in the back of the book onto the water-soluble stabilizer using the white ink transfer pen.
2. Center and pin the traced design onto a 9" square of velvet.
3. Following the stitch directions, embellish the purse front in the following order:
   - Chainstitch vines
   - Buds and leaves
   - Loopy chrysanthemums
4. Carefully tear way as much of the stabilizer as possible. Remove the remainder with a dampened cotton swab.
5. Using the pattern given, trace the purse onto the velvet, positioning the design as desired. Cut two pieces from velvet and two from the lining fabric.
6. With right sides together, sew the purse front to purse back along the sides and bottom edge. Sew the lining front to the lining back along the sides and bottom, leaving open the space between the dots for turning.
7. Place the lining and the purse pieces right sides together. Pin along the upper edges and seam together.
8. Carefully turn the purse right side out through the lining opening. Slipstitch the opening shut.
9. Press the purse on a velvet board. Tuck the upper edges of the purse into the tunnel in the frame. Sew the purse body to the frame with monofilament thread, utilizing the openwork holes in the frame. Sew twice. If desired, add beads while stitching the purse body along the top edge of the frame.
10. Sew the fringe to the front and back of the purse at the bottom, forming a double layer trim.
11. Add the chain handle to the loops located at the top of the purse frame.

ELEGANT VELVET CHAPEAU

Skill Level: Intermediate

**Techniques Highlighted: Large Spider Flower;
Simple Coiled Roses; Small Looped Flower; French Knots;
Knotted Spider Flowers; Leaves**

Grace your favorite winter ensemble with an elegant velvet hat showcasing your favorite silk ribbons and floral creations.

Materials:

- Vogue #9082—View B or comparable hat pattern
- Velvet fabric, lining fabric and cording—yardage as per pattern
- Monofilament thread
- All-purpose thread for bobbin—color matched to fashion fabric
- Stiletto, long tweezers or large needle
- Assorted 4mm and 7mm silk ribbons

Directions:

1. Cut the hat and lining from the fabric according to the pattern directions.
2. Assemble the outer hat sections and set aside.
3. Sew the crown lining to the velvet underbrim. Press.
4. Divide the brim into four equal sections. Pin mark the center half to contain the embroidery.
5. Pin mark 4" up from the bottom, non-seamed edge of the brim. This will become the fold-up portion of the hat front and the area on which all the ribbon embroidery will be stitched.
6. Referring to the design given in the back of the book, begin to stitch the silk embroidery. Because all the flowers are free form and are not anchored by vines, they can be sewn in any order and positioned at will. Flowers in the sample hat are:
   - Large Spider Flower
   - Simple Coiled Roses with leaves
   - Small Loop Flowers with French knots and beaded centers
   - Knotted Spider Flowers
7. After the embroidery is completed, assemble the hat according to the pattern directions. If desired, add small beads to the entire hat brim for visual interest.

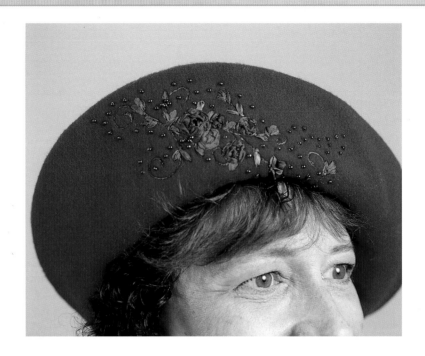

ROSES IN BURGUNDY WOOL HAT

Skill Level: Beginner

**Techniques Highlighted: Simple Coiled Rose;
Buds and Leaves, Leaves**

This handsomely-styled wide brimmed hat invites an elegant addition of silk ribbon flowers!

Materials:

- Vogue #9082—view A or comparable hat pattern
- Wool fabric, satin lining and fusible interfacing—yardage as per pattern
- Monofilament thread
- All-purpose thread on bobbin—color matched to fashion fabric
- Long tweezers, stiletto or large needle
- Iron-on silk ribbon design by Bucilla—"April Delight" #33549
- Green topstitching thread
- Assorted 4mm and 7mm silk ribbons
- Small burgundy beads
- Water-soluble stabilizer
- White ink transfer pen

Directions:

1. Cut out the hat pattern pieces from the wool fabric. Fuse the interfacing to the hat sections according to the pattern directions.
2. Transfer the design onto the stabilizer using the White Ink/ Water-Soluble Stabilizer Method described in Chapter 4.
3. Pin the traced stabilizer onto the hat brim where desired.
4. Following the manufacturer's directions, stitch the design on the right side of the fabric. Refer to Chapter 9, "April Delight" vest for the embroidery details.

MIXED MEDIA: SILK RIBBON, FREE-MOTION EMBROIDERY AND BEADING

Blend your new found silk ribbon expertise with simple machine embroidery and beading to create stunning works of art. No artistic skills? Not a problem! Look to your favorite crafts store for a tempting array of silk-screened needlework kits to use as your canvas. Originally designed for hand stitching with heavy yarns, these kits feature a design silk-screened onto cloth, with blank areas left open for handwork. The blank areas are perfect for machine worked, fill-in stitching techniques. You'll be delighted with the visual and textural effects achieved by the smooth look of free-motion machine embroidery contrasted by the loopy texture of silk ribbons and the pearly glow of beads.

Free-Motion Machine Embroidery

Free-motion embroidery is sewing with the feed dogs down on fabric which is tightly stretched in a hoop. The sewer controls the stitch length and width by moving the hoop back and forth or left and right. Simple straight or zig-zag stitches can produce satiny blocks of color.

Basic Machine Set-Up:

- Needle thread: 100% rayon or cotton embroidery thread
- Bobbin thread: 100% cotton or fine embroidery thread
- Upper tension: Slightly lowered
- Feed dogs: Disengaged or lowered
- Needle/size: Embroidery needle—#75 or higher
- Presser foot: Standard darning or open darning foot
- Wooden embroidery hoop with inner ring wrapped with twill tape
- Tear-away stabilizer support underneath area to be embroidered

Place your hands on the hoop in the 3 o'clock and 9 o'clock positions.

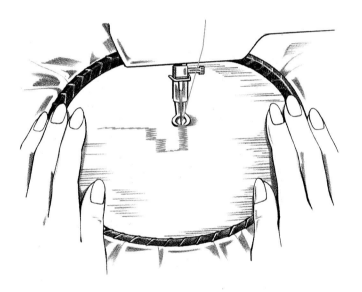

 Place a pillow under each elbow to raise them to a comfortable level avoiding shoulder and back strain!

Sit straight up and over your work with your elbows resting at an even level with the bed of your sewing machine.

Free motion work is relaxing and enjoyable, but needs a little warm up! Practice on a scrap until you feel comfortable. Simple fill-in stitches are created in one of two ways:

Straight stitch embroidery: With your hands in the correct positions, select a straight stitch and slowly move the hoop back and forth to fill in an area. When complete, create a knot by sewing in place three to four times. Snip the threads tails close to the work.

Zig-zag embroidery: Select a medium width (2.5 – 3.0mm) zig-zag stitch. Moving the hoop back to front will create a horizontal satin stitch appearing in blocks of color, while moving from side to side will form a linear straight stitch fill-in. At the end, return to a straight stitch and sew in place three to four times to knot. Clip the thread tails.

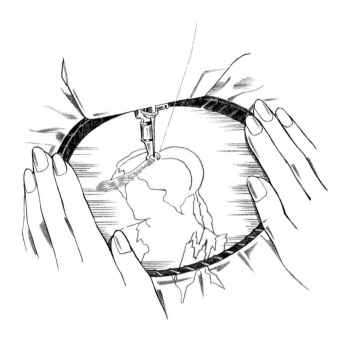

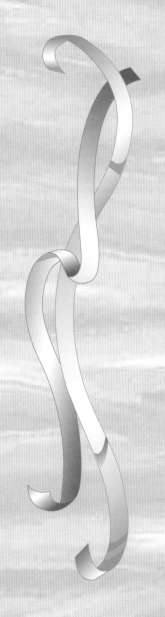

Silk Ribbon Embellishment

Accent your canvas with a garden full of silk flowers using any or all of the bobbinwork and couching techniques discussed in Chapters 5 and 6. Sewn singly or in sets, these silk additions lend visual and textural interest, contrasting against the flatter appearance of the free-motion work. Remember to tie off or fuse down the ribbon tails on the wrong side of the canvas, taking care not to pull too tightly when knotting on the underside.

Simple Beading

An elegant finishing touch can easily be added to your work with simple machine beading.

Basic Machine Set-Up:

- Needle thread: Monofilament
- Bobbin thread: 100% cotton
- Upper tension: Normal
- Feed dogs: Lowered
- Needle size: #70 or to pass through the eye of the bead
- Presser foot: None
- Beads: Size 2mm or appropriate to design

Place the area of fabric to be beaded in a hoop. Scatter a few loose beads within the hoop to pick up while stitching. Remember to lower the presser foot lever to engage the upper tension. Sew three or four times in place at the first beading site. Raise the needle, move one bead in place and sew through the hole once, then on the side of the bead. Repeat this procedure for a total of two times in and out of bead.

Sew to the next bead location. Repeat the securing process, continuing to add beads. Sew three or four times past the last bead location to create a knot. Clip the tails close to the work.

The two needlework canvases displayed in this chapter showcase two different ways to embellish with silk ribbons.

"Springtime Elegance" by Dimensions, Inc.

This lovely Victorian lady cradles a bouquet of freshly picked flowers worked in silk ribbon bobbinwork. Filler embroidery on the hat, gown and flower branches are all sewn using free-motion embroidery techniques and a combination of cotton and rayon embroidery threads. Bobbinwork flowers created using the Daisy/ Star stitch, in 4mm wide silk ribbon, replace those indicated for hand stitches. The hem detail on the dress consists of couched 4mm silk ribbon and machine-stitched pearls.

"Wiltshire Garden" by Dimensions, Inc.

This project explores your sewing machine's built-in stitch capabilities. While some areas of the canvas are filled in by free-motion embroidery, others utilize the most basic built-in patterns in new and creative ways. Short bursts of satin stitches make ideal bricks on the garden gate, elongated satin stitched ovals become leaves, and spiky decorative stitches, sewn at a shortened stitch length simulate grass. All "Wiltshire Garden" silk ribbon embellishment is created using couching techniques. The rose-strewn garden gate consists of many, many French knots. Floral clusters on the left foreground are simple Lazy Daisy's sewn at differing sizes using a variety of ribbons.

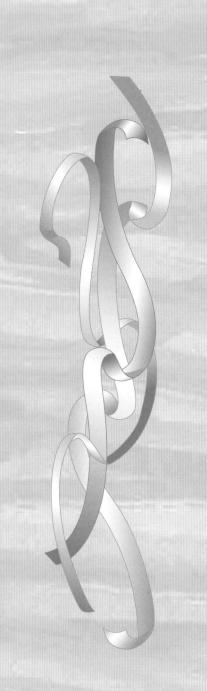

"SPRINGTIME ELEGANCE"
by Dimensions, Inc.

Advanced

**Techniques Highlighted: Free-Motion Embroidery;
Silk Ribbon Flowers of choice**

Materials:

- Silk-screened crewel embroidery needlework kit
- Fusible interfacing as large as canvas
- Tear-away stabilizer as large as canvas
- Fade-away fabric marker

- Wooden embroidery hoop with inner ring wrapped with twill tape
- Assorted rayon or cotton embroidery threads—color matched to yarns included in kit
- Assorted sizes and colors of silk ribbons
- Monofilament thread
- 100% cotton embroidery thread for bobbin
- Embroidery needles—#75 – #80

Directions:

1. Prepare the needlework canvas by steaming it flat. Stabilize the canvas by fusing interfacing to the wrong side. Pin the tear-away stabilizer to the wrong side of the canvas.
2. Locate the stitching chart in the needlework kit. Match and write down the embroidery thread colors on the chart. This will provide a quick reference for colors while sewing. Review the sample given in the back of the book for the "Springtime Elegance" needlework canvas. Place the stitching chart and color photo of the completed canvas near your sewing machine.

 The tear-away stabilizer will remain on the canvas after stitching and will not be removed.

3. Wind two or three bobbins of cotton bobbin thread to have handy during project.
4. Place a section of the canvas to be embroidered in a hoop. The project shown in this book was stitched in this order:
   ▌ Large areas: Free motion embroidery
   ▌ Florals: Silk ribbon embroidery
   ▌ Fill in: Free motion embroidery
   ▌ Beaded accents as desired
5. Thread the machine with the first color selected, rayon in the needle and cotton in the bobbin. Attach an open or standard darning foot to your machine and lower the feed dogs.
6. Consult the stitching chart and use a fade-away marker to color in the areas to be embroidered in the first color.
7. Position the hooped canvas under the presser foot. Lower the presser foot lever to engage the upper tension and prevent "thread nests" on the wrong side. Take one stitch, pulling on the needle thread tail to draw the bobbin thread to the top. Stitch over both thread tails three or four times to secure. Clip the tails.
8. Reset the machine for either a straight or a medium-width zig-zag stitch. Begin to fill in the areas colored by stitching at an even speed. Remember that this type of sewing is very forgiving. If you move the hoop too fast or unevenly, you can easily sew back to the bare spots and fill in. As each section is completed, finish by sewing in place three or four times with a straight stitch. Clip the thread tails.
9. When all the large areas are embroidered, add your favorite silk ribbon florals using built-in stitches, bobbinwork or by couching the ribbons down from the top. Don't worry if your silk flowers are not covering the canvas blanks entirely, these areas can be easily filled in with additional free-motion embroidery.
10. Add simple beading to the canvas for a finishing touch.

A Note on Finishing

After your embellished canvas is complete, invest your time in finding a professional needlework framer to frame your work. Repetitive hoopings and the added weight of embroidery threads and ribbons can distort even the most well-prepared canvas. A good framer will not only eliminate the bumps and wrinkles, but square up your canvas to

respectability. Reputable frame shops carry extra rigid needlework mounting boards not easily found by the home sewer, not to mention a wealth of tempting and unique frame and mat styles.

Treat yourself to a beautiful framing job—you and your embroidered work deserve it!

ADDITIONAL STITCHES

Once you've had fun sewing the designs discussed in the previous chapters, you'll want to create more and more projects. The number of designs possible by combining simple loops, twirls and folds is limited only by your imagination. Look at the wealth of patterns available in traditional handwork silk ribbon publications. With a little practice, you'll soon be able to dissect traditional handwork patterns into sewing machine applications.

On the following pages is a collection of a dozen more beautiful florals and little critters to get you started. You'll be able to design endless combinations by using different ribbon widths or textures. Choose a variegated ribbon instead of a solid, add a spark with a sheer organza, or try the subtle shading of a hand-dyed length of ribbon. Have fun!

All the following silk ribbon patterns have the same basic machine set-up. First the fabric is stretched tightly in a hoop. Put monofilament thread in the needle and all purpose thread in the bobbin. The feed dogs are lowered and the Needle Stop/down is engaged, if available. The presser foot lever is lowered engaging the upper tension.

At the beginning of each pattern, the threads are secured by taking one stitch. Pull on the needle thread to draw the bobbin thread to the top. With both threads in one hand, sew three or four stitches close together to lock the threads in the fabric. Clip the thread tails close to the work.

Silky
Sunflower

TIP: An open toe
embroidery foot
gives best visibility
for this method.

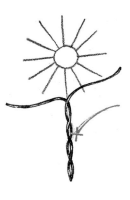

Stem: The stem and branch are sewn
using the cross-cross chainstitch and
topstitching thread instead of ribbon. Begin
to sew the stem from the base to the top,
the branch from the stem out, leaving tails
to be covered by silk ribbon embroidery.

Leaf: Use the loop method from the Lazy Daisy to couch down one petal using 4mm silk ribbon.

Petals: Beginning at the center circle, sew the first loop to the petal top, tack two times. Sew back to the center circle, bringing ribbon down as flat as possible. Tack.

Pivot and sew additional petals to complete flower. Clip the tail. To help petals lie down flat, sew around the center circle two times.

The center is filled with French knots or small beads.

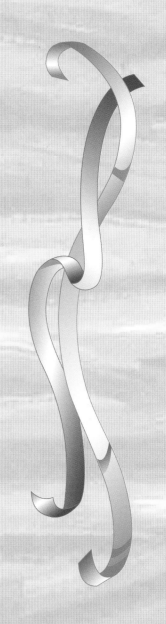

Embroidered Lazy Daisy

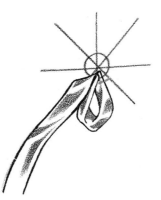

Petals: Draw an eight-petaled Lazy Daisy with a small circle at the center. Secure 4mm or 7mm ribbon at the bottom of the center circle at the 6 o'clock position where the circle meets the center drawn line.

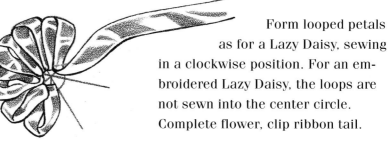

Form looped petals as for a Lazy Daisy, sewing in a clockwise position. For an embroidered Lazy Daisy, the loops are not sewn into the center circle. Complete flower, clip ribbon tail.

To complete the center embroidery, thread the needle with a decorative thread. Fill in the center by moving the hoop in a circular motion, adding veins with free-motion straight stitching.

Pansy

Leaves: Couch two horizontal loops (left and right) at the center.

Petals: Couch three large loops at the top of the flower in a dark color. Couch two smaller loops at the flower bottom in a lighter tone of the same color.

Veins: Raise the feed dogs and thread the machine with yellow thread. Using an open embroidery foot, sew three centered veins on the top petals and two on the lower petals. Switch to black thread and sew slightly shorter veins in the same places.

Hollyhock

Stem: Raise the feed dogs and sew a criss-cross chainstitch using topstitching thread and an open embroidery foot. Sew the stem from the bottom to the top.

Leaves: Lower the feed dogs. With silk ribbon, couch down leaves with single loops.

Buds: Sew four to six French knots at the top in green ribbon to simulate unopened buds.

 TIP: Fewer buds can be sewn to allow more stem to show. Add additional leaves at the flower base, if necessary.

Flowers: Fill the remaining stem with French knots sewn in the color of silk ribbon of choice.

Marigold

Stem: Raise the feed dogs. Stitch the stem using the criss-cross chainstitch and topstitching thread. Use an open embroidery foot. Sew stem from bottom to top.

Leaves: Lower the feed dogs. Sew the leaves using single couched loops and silk ribbon.

Petals: Couch the first layer of petals as done on the Silky Sunflower, bringing loops to meet in the center.

Couch six smaller petals on top of the first petals, tacking them down only in the center. Secure the petals in the flower center and clip the tail close.

Center: Embellish with ribbon French knots or small beads.

Ferns and Fillers

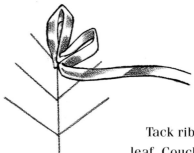

Constructed entirely of ribbon, these stems can be used singly with flowers, or clustered together to form bushes. I find them easier to sew from the top down to the base.

Tack ribbon down at the base of the top leaf. Couch one looped leaf at this site, returning to the center stem. Tack the ribbon down at the stem. Sew down to the next leaf pair site, keeping ribbon free. Sew a looped leaf to the right, then to the right, again returning to the center stem. Tack ribbon at the stem.

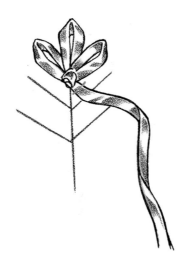

Sew down to the next leaf pair site. Bring flat ribbon down, tack, then sew two more looped leaves. After each pair of leaves is secured add a French knot on the stem line.

Once the leaf is as large as desired, secure the ribbon at the base of the stem.

Ruched Ribbons

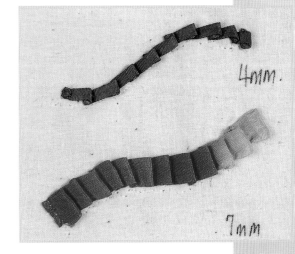

This beautiful filler stitch looks harder than it really is. Use it in place of leaves, or stems, formed into pleated bows, or wherever a space needs an interesting fill of ribbon.

Mark a line to follow while stitching. Draw intersecting lines indicating where ribbon is to be tacked to create pleats. Press under ½" at the ribbon end. Tack the pressed end down at the beginning point of your drawn line.

Keeping the ribbon free, sew to the next intersecting line. Raise the needle. Keeping ribbon flat, insert a stiletto or seam ripper underneath the ribbon. Pull the looped, flat ribbon backwards halfway up the previously sewn loop. Sew the flat ribbon in place at the marking. Continue sewing to the marked lines, looping and tacking the ribbon in place until design is completed.

Secure the ends. Press the loops lightly to one side to conceal stitches and create a pleated effect.

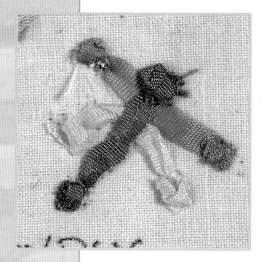

Fantasy Firefly

Wings: Secure the ribbon at one wing end, sew a French knot at the wing tip to conceal the cut ribbon end. Tack the flat ribbon at the center, continuing on to other end, finishing with a French knot. Clip tail. Sew the second wing in the same manner.

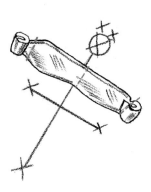

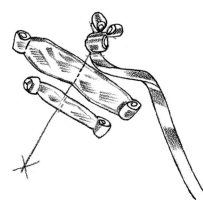

Body: Secure the ribbon at the head site. Sew the head with a French knot, bringing the ribbon flat onto body.

 TIP: French knots may be eliminated and small glass beads be substituted instead.

Tack the ribbon at the base of the head, over wings, traveling down to the tail. Finish the tail with a French knot. Clip the ribbon close to the work.

Ladybug

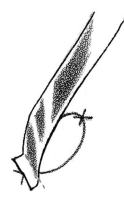

Body: Couch a single Lazy Daisy loop for body.

Head, Antennae and Dots: Thread the machine with black all-purpose thread. Free-motion embroider a small circle for head, straight lines for antennae. Sew tiny dots on top of body to finish.

Bumblebee

Wings: Couch down two small loops for wings, beginning and ending at the center.

Body: Couch down one slightly larger loop for body.

Head, Stripes and Stinger: Thread your machine with all-purpose black thread. Free-motion embroider a small circle for the head. Straight stitch stripes on the body and make a stinger.

Butterfly

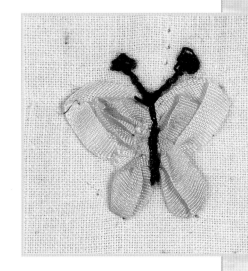

Wings: Couch down two outer loops creating the upper wings, leaving a space for additional ribbon.

Using a second color, couch down two inner loops on upper wings, and two loops on lower half.

Head, Antennae and Body: Thread the machine with black all-purpose thread and free-motion embroider the head, antennae at the top and body between wings.

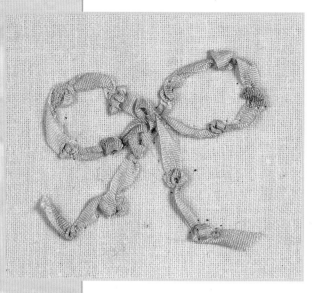

Knotted Bow

Tack ribbon at "X" with a ¼"
tail extending. Sew a French
knot, bringing ribbon around
knot in the direction you are
sewing the remainder of the
bow. Tack flat ribbon in place.

Keeping the ribbon free, sew
to the next desired knot location
and tack the ribbon in place. Sew
another French knot, again
bringing ribbon in the direction
of the sewing.

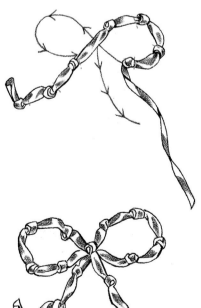

Continue sewing bow and
knots following directions on the
area for continuous, unbroken
bow construction.

Looped and Tacked Bow

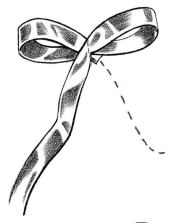

Secure the ribbon at the bow center. Loop the ribbon and tack in center to form left side of bow, repeat for right side of bow.

Trail the end of the ribbon from the bow center to form the left streamer, tacking where desired. Finish bow end with a French knot.

Attach a second piece of ribbon between the bow loops, sew a French knot to conceal the tail. Loop to form right streamer, tacking as desired and finishing with a French knot. Clip ends close.

Chapter Nine

A GALLERY OF SILK RIBBON VESTS

Enjoy experimenting with your own designs and stitch combinations to create unique art-to-wear!

Display your newly-found silk ribbon expertise on the sewer's favorite canvas—the vest! This wearable-art gallery features four vests embellished with silk ribbon bobbinwork and couching, using stitch and flower techniques discussed in previous chapters. The fifth vest demonstrates a clever application of your scraps, those bits of silk ribbon too pretty and a bit too long to throw way. Both purchased and machine sewn vests were used. Where to start? The choice is yours.

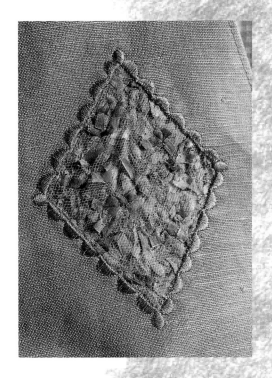

"APRIL DELIGHT"

This purchased pink silk noil vest is embellished using ribbons and topstitching threads, all couched from the top. Bucilla Corporation's Beginner's Level iron-on transfer design, #33549 "April Delight," designed for handwork techniques is translated into machine application.

Directions:

1. Pink the edges piece of a piece of fusible tricot interfacing and fuse to the back of the desired embroidery area on the vest. Before fusing, lift any facings away from the garment so that they don't get caught in the fusing process and create a bulky ridge line on the garment front.

2. Following manufacturer's instructions, cut out and iron on the design onto the vest. Place the area of the vest to be embellished into an embroidery hoop keeping the fabric as taut as possible.

3. Refer to the manufacturer's embroidery diagram for suggestions on thread color placement and stitch selection. Compare their suggestions to the stitches and flowers discussed in the previous chapters. Create a ledger for yourself of your thread and stitch choices.

4. This entire design was stitched from the right side or top of the garment. The embroidery was completed in the following order:

   Stems and Vines: Use the criss-cross chainstitch, replacing the topstitching thread with silk ribbon.

   Buds and Leaves: Machine stitch all sections of the design indicated for the Lazy Daisy Stitch, the Straight Stitch and the Japanese Ribbon Stitch using the Simple Buds and Leaves directions from Chapter 6.

   Roses: Follow the directions for the Simple Coiled Rose in Chapter 6. Stitch roses in two sizes for visual interest.

   French Knots: Finish your design with French Knots as outlined in Chapter 6 or replace the knots with pearls or beads.

"FLOWERS AND VINES"

Trailing vines and silk ribbon blooms tumble across this machine-sewn linen vest. Designed with a combination of vines created with your sewing machine's built-in stitches, as well as silk ribbon bobbinwork, you'll enjoy the textural interest that develops while stitching. Let your machine do all the work while creating these unique motifs!

Directions:

1. Cut out the vest fronts from your fashion fabric. Fuse tricot interfacing to the entire left and right front vest pieces.
2. Using a fade-away fabric marker, draw lines to follow for the machine-sewn vines on the right side of the vest fronts. Select an appropriate built-in stitch on your sewing machine and embroider on the right side of both vest fronts, using rayon or metallic embroidery threads.
3. The remainder of the vest is sewn from the wrong side, using silk ribbon bobbinwork and the techniques and stitches suggested in Chapter 5.

Silk Ribbon Vines: Using a straight or feather stitch, sew silk ribbon bobbinwork vines, entwining them with the previously sewn machine stitched vines. You'll be able to see the bobbin thread from the machine stitched designs on the wrong side while you are sewing. Pivot and turn your work accordingly for a pleasing look.

Silk Ribbon Flowers: Fill in your vines with beautiful silk ribbon buds, made doubly attractive since your machine does all the work. The flowers on this vest were stitched entirely using the built-in Star/Daisy stitch. Sew the flowers singly or in clusters.

Finishing Silk Ribbon Embroidery: Using a large-eyed tapestry needle, pull all thread tails to the wrong side of the vest fronts. Knot together or fuse the ends down. Press the two front sections from the wrong side and continue assembling your vest.

 TIP: Use a tear-away stabilizer on the wrong side of the fabric and the machine embroidery to support the stitches and prevent puckering.

"SUNFLOWER GARDEN"

Bright sunflowers, colorful butterflies, busy ladybugs and other critters border this purchased, navy linen vest. Take advantage of your built-in machine stitches to sew background fillers such as grass and bugs. Silk ribbon threads couched from the top adds flowers and other delights. Once you start stitching your garden, it's hard to stop!

Directions:

1. Carefully remove any vest pockets from the front sections, if necessary. Apply a 3½" wide band of fusible tricot interfacing, approximately 1½" from the hem edge, to the wrong side of

the vest along the front and back. This interfacing will help support both the machine and silk ribbon embroidery.

2. Using a fade-away fabric marker on lighter-colored fabrics or a soapstone marker on darker colors, draw a continuous, slightly curved line on the right side around the entire bottom of the vest, approximately $1\frac{1}{2}$" above the hem edge. Follow this line for the "grass" embroidery.

Grass: Select a stitch that has one straight edge and an irregular pattern on the opposite edge for the "grass". A compact edging stitch was used on the sample. Place a tear-away stabilizer underneath the drawn line and embroider "grass" using your sewing machine. Tear-away the stabilizer after the embroidery is complete.

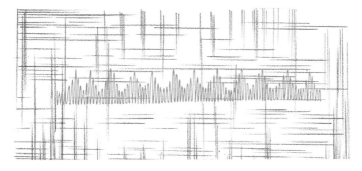

Sunflowers: Trace the sunflower design trio onto the right side of the vest following the design in the back of the book and spacing accordingly. Place the vest area to be embroidered in a hoop. Sew in the stems using the criss-cross chainstitch from Chapter 6 and topstitching thread. Embroider the center sunflower and leaves following the directions for the Silky Sunflower in Chapter 8. The smaller sunflowers on either side are created using the same techniques for petals, stems and leaves. The bases of the side sunflowers are filled in using free-motion embroidery techniques and green rayon thread. Refer to Chapter 7, Mixed Media, for free-motion embroidery directions.

3. Fill in the garden scene with ladybugs and butterflies. Refer to the Additional Stitches found in Chapter 8 for more details on creating bugs and critters.

 TIP: The topiary tree design, by itself, can be stitched on linen and framed for a visually interesting and textural picture.

"ROSEBUD TOPIARY"

Silk ribbon embroidery, pin weaving and machine satin stitching all work hand-in-hand to create a charming rosebud tree on this machine sewn vest. A free-form cascade of roses and buds balance out the opposite side of the vest, while a rose adorned stay finishes the vest back.

Directions:

1. Cut vest fronts from the fashion fabric of your choice. Interface both front pieces with fusible tricot interfacing. Transfer the topiary design found in the back of the book to the lower section of the right front using any one of the transferring techniques mentioned in Chapter 4.

   All embroidery on this vest is stitched on the right side of the fabric.

2. **Satin Stitched Trunk:** The tree trunk is created by stitching two rows of satin stitching next to each other using two slightly different widths. Straight stitching is then added to the left and right outer edges of the satin stitching giving the trunk a more defined and polished look.

   Thread your machine with brown rayon thread. Set your machine for a 6mm wide satin stitch. Place tear-away stabilizer underneath the trunk area and sew. Increase your stitch width to 6½mm and satin stitch a second time. This second row of stitching will create a slightly padded, dense, rich look to the trunk. Straight stitch on the left and right edges of the trunk to enhance.

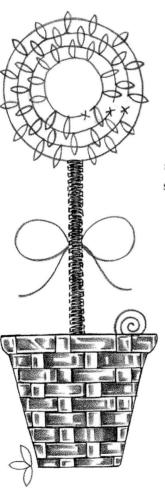

3. **Pin Woven Basket:** Cut and pin a 3½" square of fusible tricot interfacing to a pin weaving or grided pressboard, with the fusible side facing up. Cut and pin lengths of 4mm wide silk ribbon horizontally across the interfacing, edges butted, covering the entire piece of interfacing. Begin weaving vertical rows, over and under the previous rows of ribbon.

From the right side, carefully fuse the ribbons to the interfacing with a dry iron. Remove the pins and press again on the right side. Turn the pin weaving over and press once more on the wrong side to secure. Trace the basket shape onto the pin woven "fabric" and cut out. Place the basket shape in place and satin stitch around the outer edge to secure.

4. **Rosebud Topiary Tree Top:** Leaves on the tree top are created using a long length of 4mm silk ribbon tacked into a continuous circle of loops. Tack down the ribbon tail at any point on the outer edge of the drawn circle. Using the "Buds" technique in Chapter 6, tack down one bud. Drag the ribbon to a point on the circle approximately ¼" - ½" away from the first bud and tack down a second bud. Continue creating buds and dragging ribbon until the entire circle is completed. Begin the second row like the first, tacking down the tail of a ribbon and creating buds. Position these buds between the buds stitched in the first row to fill in the tree. Continue around the second, third, and fourth circles, and so on, until the tree is filled.

 TIP: Don't worry about any gaps in the tree as these spaces can be filled in with rosebuds. Add interest to the tree top by varying leaf colors or using hand-dyed ribbons while sewing

5. **Rosebuds:** Add Simple Coiled Roses, described in Chapter 6, to the tree top where desired. Small beads can be added to the flowers' centers for interest. Position additional rosebuds and roses near the basket base.

6. **Looped and Tacked Bow:** Following the directions in Chapter 8, add a bow to the tree trunk just below the topiary section

7. Sew a free-form cascade of coiled roses and buds on a criss-cross chainstitch vine to the upper shoulder area on the left front piece.

8. Sew a trio of Simple Coiled Roses on a narrow, lined band of fabric replacing the vest back ties. Gather the vest center back by sewing a piece of elastic between the lining and vest. Sew the decorated band on top of the elastic shirring, securing it on each end with the same buttons that close the vest front.

"CONFETTI SCRAPS"

What a wonderful way to use up those precious, tiny bits of silk ribbon! Snippets of brightly colored ribbon are trapped between layers of tulle and stitched together to create ribbon fabric. Applied to a purchased vest using a reverse appliqué technique, they create colorful peek-a-book windows of color.

Directions:

1. Trace and cut out the diamond shape given in the Patterns or draw any shape desired onto paper. Pin the shape(s) in place on the vest to determine exact placement. Once you have finalized your design, outline the shapes onto the right and wrong side of the garment using the appropriate marking tool.

2. **Ribbon Fabric**: Cut two 9" squares of tulle. Snip small pieces of leftover silk ribbons onto one piece of the tulle, keeping the bits fairly centered within a 6-6½" square. After filling the space with ribbons, place the second layer of tulle over the snipped ribbon scraps. Center both tulle layers in an embroidery hoop keeping the fabric taut.

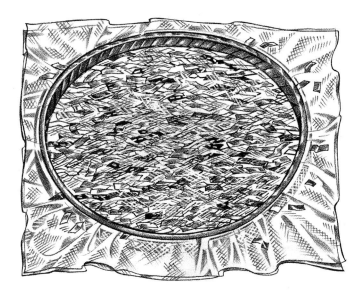

   Lower your feed dogs and secure the ribbon snips between the tulle by meander-stitching through all layers using monofilament thread in the needle and all-purpose thread in the bobbin. Sew until most of the ribbon snips have been stitched at least once. To add visual interest and texture, sprinkle additional ribbon scraps on top of the top layer of tulle and stitch in place. Remove the fabric from the hoop and press flat.

3. **Reverse Appliqué Ribbon Diamond:** Pin the ribbon fabric over the traced diamond on the wrong side of the vest making sure that the section with the most ribbon sewn down is centered within the diamond. From the right side, straight stitch the tulle fabric to the vest front along the traced lines. Stitch a second row close to the first around the entire diamond.

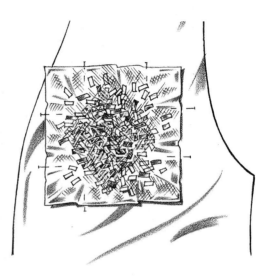

Carefully cut away the diamond center from the vest fabric with appliqué scissors, being careful not to cut into the tulle. Carefully cut away the tulle from outside the diamond shape on the inside of the vest.

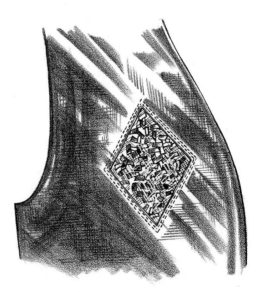

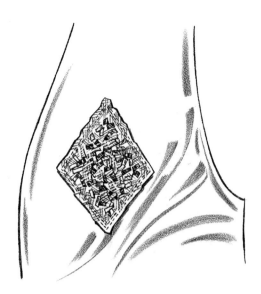

Select a satin stitch pattern on your sewing machine that
has one straight and one shaped edge, for example, a half oval,
half circle, or half diamond. Using rayon thread, stitch these
half patterns on the right side around the ribbon fabric window,
securing and embellishing the outer edges in one sewing.

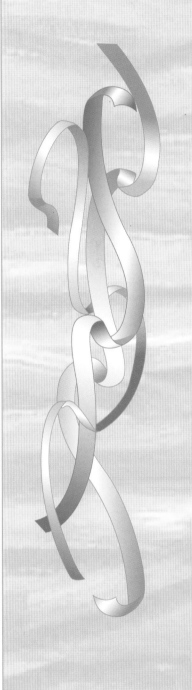

ABOUT THE AUTHOR

Nancy Bednar is a free-lance sewing specialist, training consultant and writer. She is a regular contributor to **Sewing Update** and **Serger Update** newsletters, and was featured in the Holiday '95 issue of **Sewing Decor** magazine, all published by PJS. Nancy has contributed to **Sew News** and a variety of books such as: *Wardrobe Quick Fixes* by Jan Saunders; *Travel Gear and Gifts to Make* and *More Sweatshirts With Style*, both by Mary Mulari; and the newly published *The Experts Book of Sewing Tips and Techniques* by Rodale. As a free-lance training consultant for Bernina of America, she has developed educational materials, tested new products and conducted seminars across the United States for dealers and consumers alike.

METRIC EQUIVALENTS

INCHES TO MILLIMETERS AND CENTIMETERS
MM—millimeters   CM—centimeters

Inches	MM	CM	Inches	CM	Inches	CM
1/8	3	0.3	9	22.9	30	76.2
1/4	6	0.6	10	25.4	31	78.7
3/8	10	1.0	11	27.9	32	81.3
1/2	13	1.3	12	30.5	33	83.8
5/8	16	1.6	13	33.0	34	86.4
3/4	19	1.9	14	35.6	35	88.9
7/8	22	2.2	15	38.1	36	91.4
1	25	2.5	16	40.6	37	94.0
1 1/4	32	3.2	17	43.2	38	96.5
1 1/2	38	3.8	18	45.7	39	99.1
1 3/4	44	4.4	19	48.3	40	101.6
2	51	5.1	20	50.8	41	104.1
2 1/2	64	6.4	21	53.3	42	106.7
3	76	7.6	22	55.9	43	109.2
3 1/2	89	8.9	23	58.4	44	111.8
4	102	10.2	24	61.0	45	114.3
4 1/2	114	11.4	25	63.5	46	116.8
5	127	12.7	26	66.0	47	119.4
6	152	15.2	27	68.6	48	121.9
7	178	17.8	28	71.1	49	124.5
8	203	20.3	29	73.7	50	127.0

METRIC CONVERSION CHART

Yards	Inches	Meters
1/8	4.5	0.11
1/4	9	0.23
3/8	13.5	0.34
1/2	18	0.46
5/8	22.5	0.57
3/4	27	0.69
7/8	31.5	0.80
1	36	0.91
1 1/8	40.5	1.03
1 1/4	45	1.14
1 3/8	49.5	1.26
1 1/2	54	1.37
1 5/8	58.5	1.49
1 3/4	63	1.60
1 7/8	67.5	1.71
2	72	1.83

KEY TO SEWING MACHINE
TERMS & ABBREVIATIONS

SL: Stitch length

SW: Stitch width. Refer to suggested length and width of a sewn pattern. Many machines will automatically set length and width when a stitch is selected. Most auto settings, however, can be fine tuned for your desired results.

Long Stitch: A stitch function available on many sewing machines that directs the machine to sew every other stitch. In silk ribbon embroidery, this function allows the ribbon to sewn with a looser appearance, showing the ribbon to its best advantage.

Pattern Doubled: A built-in function on some machines that will increase both the width and length of a stitch equally without distorting the original design. If pattern double is not available on your machine, increase your stitch length as long as possible.

Feed Dogs Lowered: The lower feeding mechanism on the throat plate of the sewing machine is disengaged either by turning a knob or shifting a lever. Lowering the feed dogs allows the sewer to move the fabric at will, controlling stitch length, width and direction.

Upper Tension: The amount of tension placed on the needle thread as indicated by the tension dial, located on the upper portion of the sewing machine. This tension

For additional silk ribbon resources in the United States,
please send a SASE to Sewing Information Resources, Box. 330, Wasco, IL 60183.

GARDEN SAMPLER FRAMED OVAL

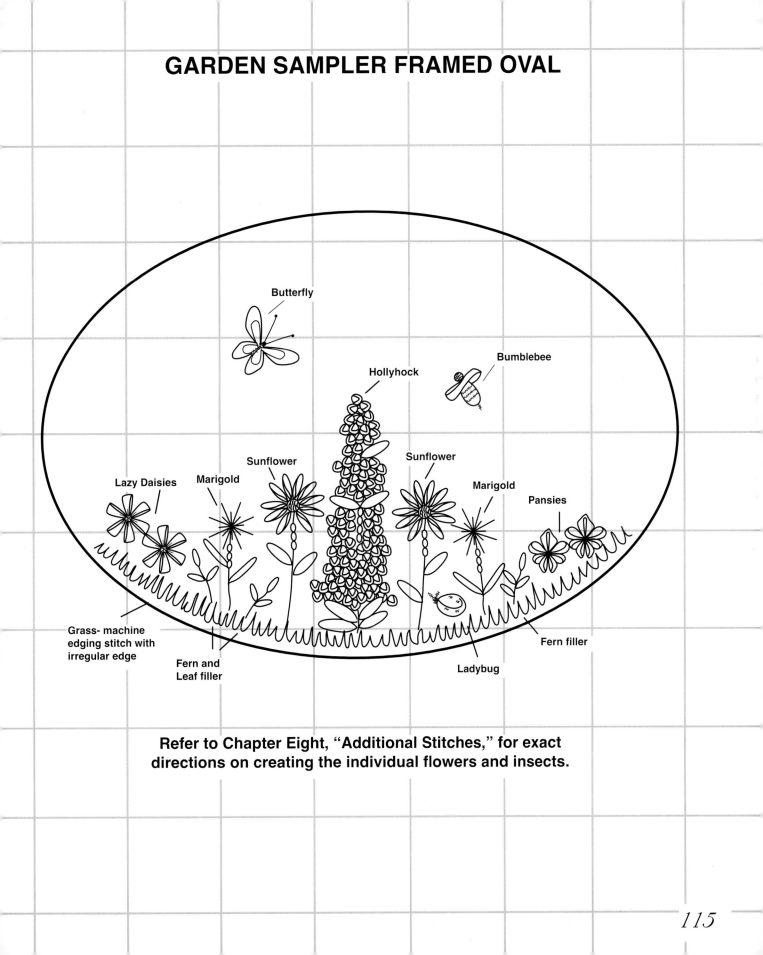

Butterfly

Bumblebee

Hollyhock

Sunflower

Sunflower

Lazy Daisies

Marigold

Marigold

Pansies

**Grass- machine
edging stitch with
irregular edge**

**Fern and
Leaf filler**

Ladybug

Fern filler

**Refer to Chapter Eight, "Additional Stitches," for exact
directions on creating the individual flowers and insects.**

WILTSHIRE GARDEN NEEDLEWORK CANVAS

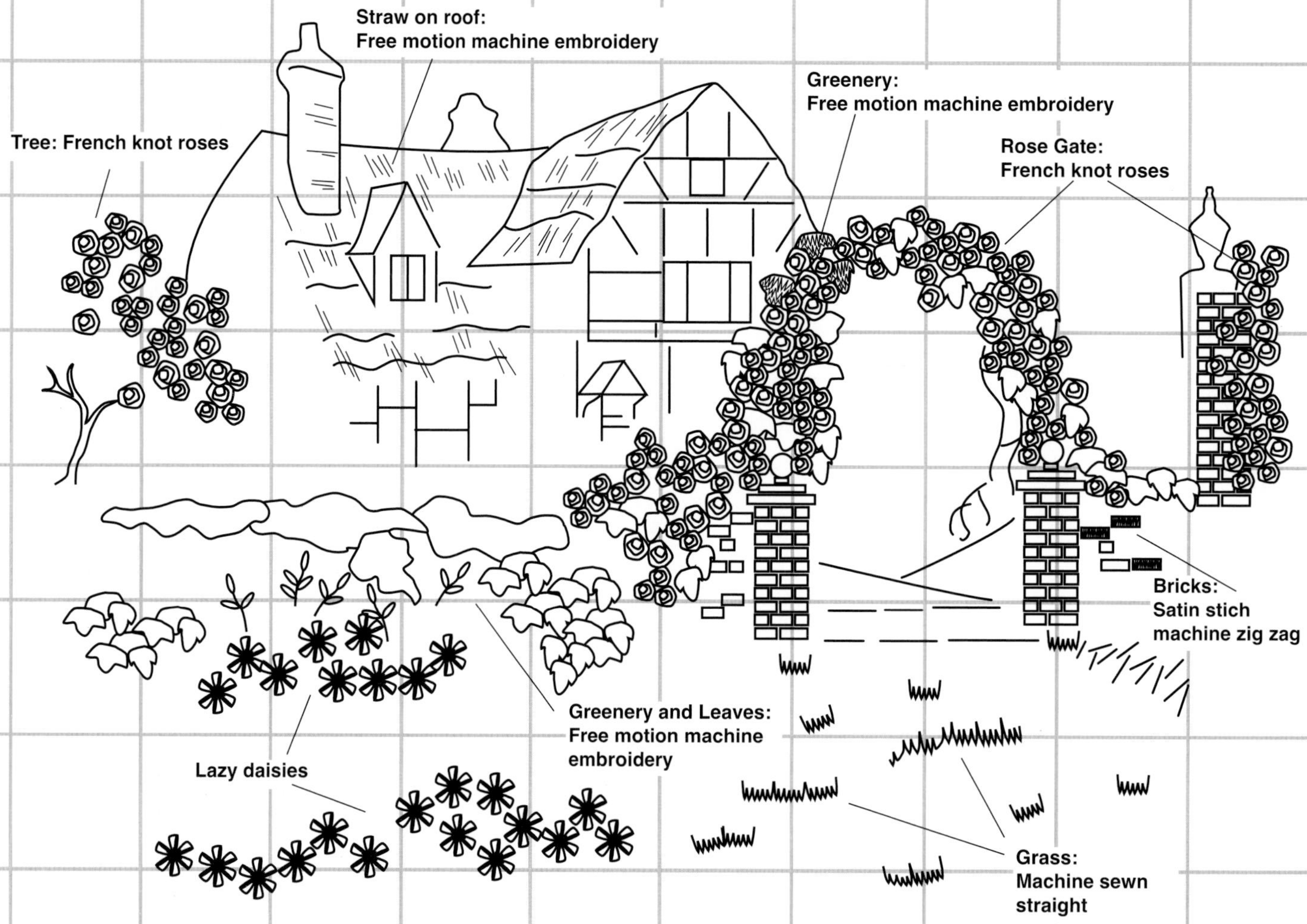

Straw on roof:
Free motion machine embroidery

Greenery:
Free motion machine embroidery

Tree: French knot roses

Rose Gate:
French knot roses

Bricks:
Satin stich
machine zig zag

Greenery and Leaves:
Free motion machine
embroidery

Lazy daisies

Grass:
Machine sewn
straight

RIBBON EMBELLISHED PHOTO ALBUM

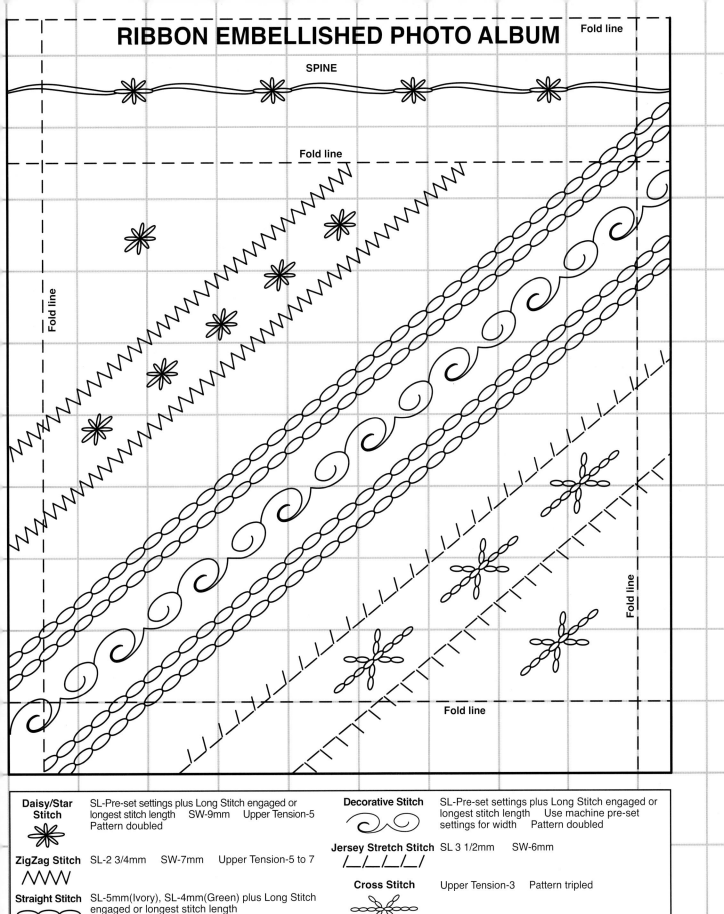

Fold line

SPINE

Fold line

Fold line

Fold line

Fold line

Daisy/Star Stitch	SL-Pre-set settings plus Long Stitch engaged or longest stitch length SW-9mm Upper Tension-5 Pattern doubled	**Decorative Stitch**	SL-Pre-set settings plus Long Stitch engaged or longest stitch length Use machine pre-set settings for width Pattern doubled
ZigZag Stitch	SL-2 3/4mm SW-7mm Upper Tension-5 to 7	**Jersey Stretch Stitch**	SL 3 1/2mm SW-6mm
Straight Stitch	SL-5mm(Ivory), SL-4mm(Green) plus Long Stitch engaged or longest stitch length	**Cross Stitch**	Upper Tension-3 Pattern tripled

ELEGANT VELVET CHAPEAU

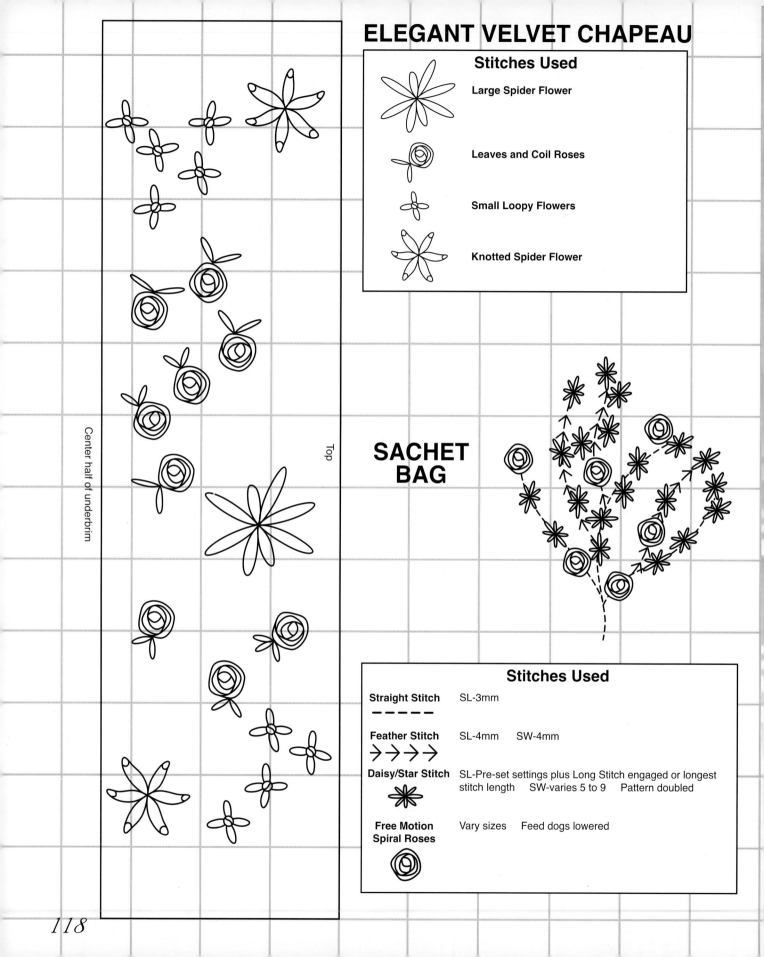

Center half of underbrim

Top

Stitches Used

Large Spider Flower

Leaves and Coil Roses

Small Loopy Flowers

Knotted Spider Flower

SACHET BAG

Stitches Used

Straight Stitch SL-3mm
– – – – –

Feather Stitch SL-4mm   SW-4mm
→ → → →

Daisy/Star Stitch SL-Pre-set settings plus Long Stitch engaged or longest
stitch length   SW-varies 5 to 9   Pattern doubled

Free Motion Spiral Roses Vary sizes   Feed dogs lowered

RIBBON EMBROIDERED PJs

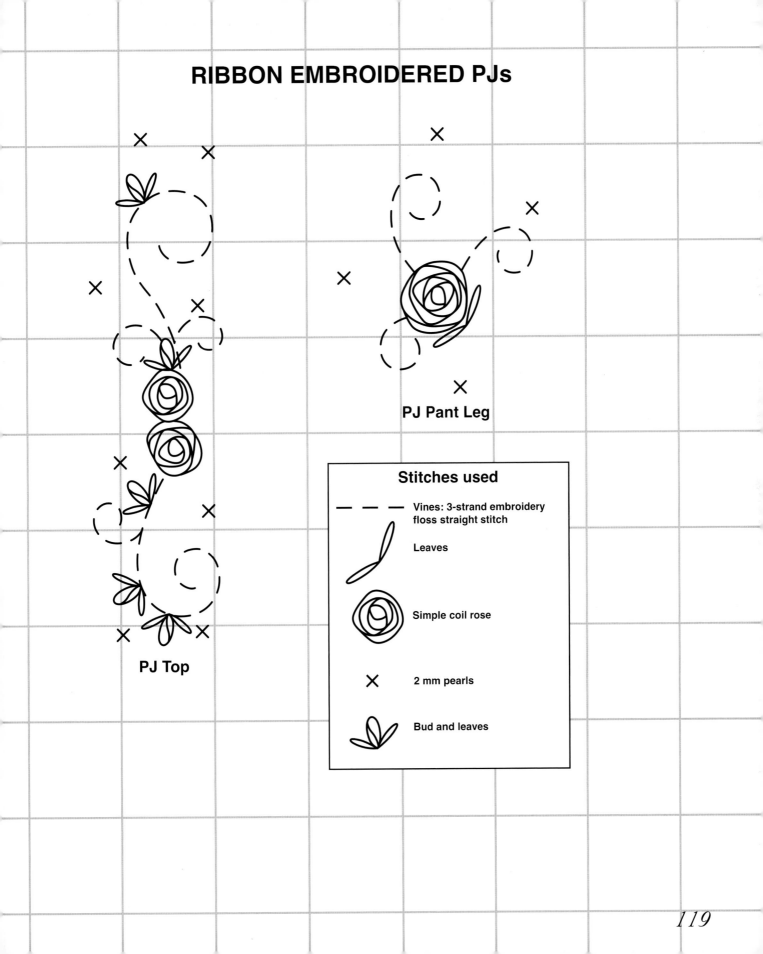

PJ Pant Leg

PJ Top

Stitches used

– – – – Vines: 3-strand embroidery floss straight stitch

Leaves

Simple coil rose

✕ 2 mm pearls

Bud and leaves

SPRINGTIME ELEGANCE NEEDLEWORK CANVAS

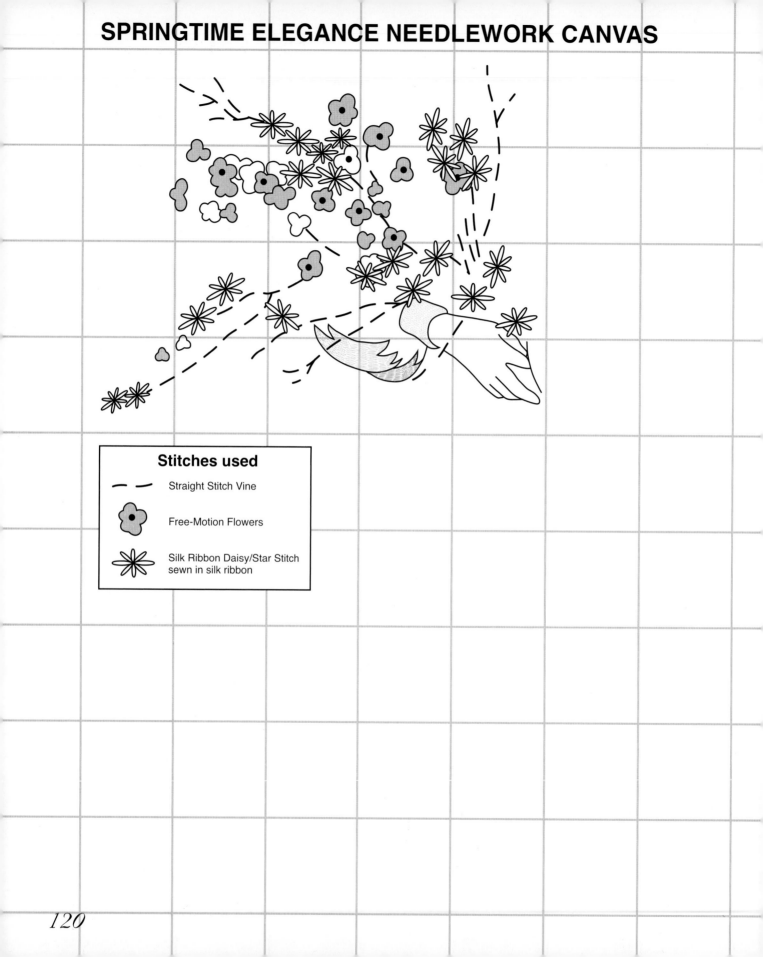

Stitches used

— — — Straight Stitch Vine

Free-Motion Flowers

Silk Ribbon Daisy/Star Stitch
sewn in silk ribbon

DAISY BARRETTE

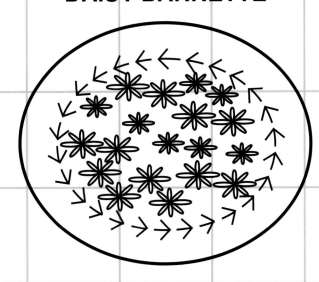

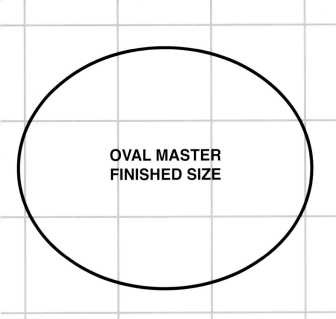

**OVAL MASTER
FINISHED SIZE**

VELVET FLORAL SPRAY

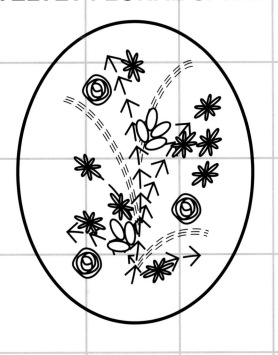

Stitches used: Daisy Barrette

Feather Stitch

SL-4mm plus Long Stitch engaged or longest stitch length   SW-5mm   Upper Tension-5   Pattern doubled   (Sewn 1/2" in from basted edge)

ZigZag/Lazy Daisy

SW-9mm   Feed dogs lowered   Needle Down engaged

ZigZag/Lazy Daisy

SW-6mm   Feed dogs lowered   Needle Down engaged

Stitches used: Velvet Floral Spray

Triple Straight Stitch

Pre-set settings using rayon and metallic threads

Feather Stitch

SL-4mm   SW-5mm   Upper Tension-5

Daisy/Star Stitch

SL-4mm plus Long Stitch engaged or longest stitch length   SW-7mm   Upper Tension-5 Pattern doubled

Free Motion Roses

Upper Tension-4   Feed dogs lowered

Seed Pearls

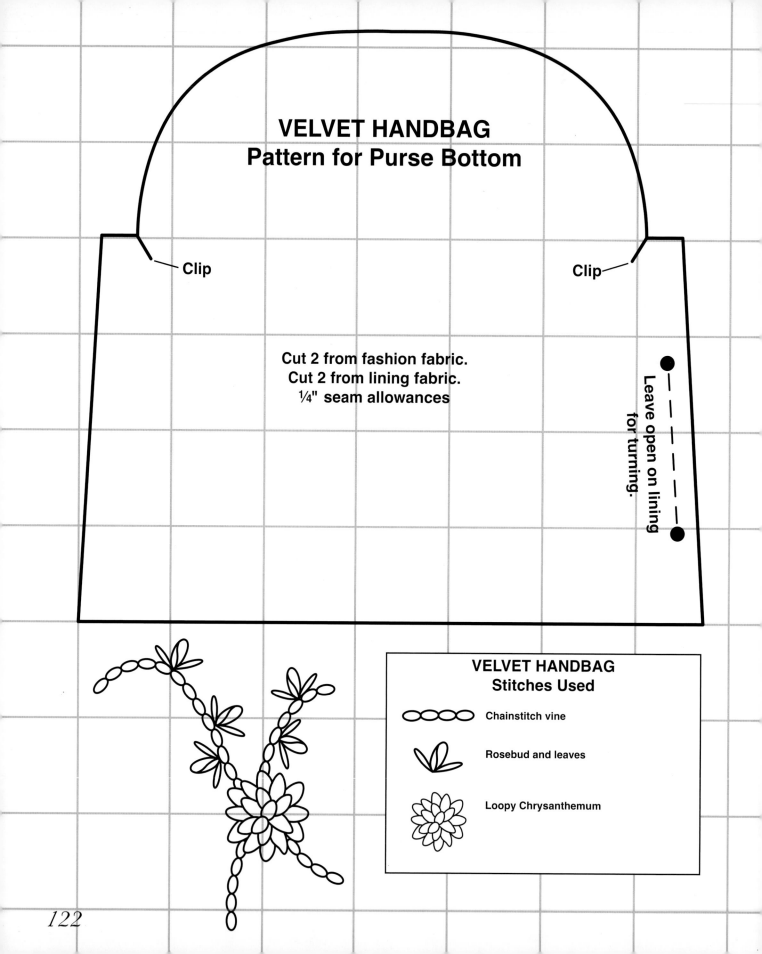

VELVET HANDBAG
Pattern for Purse Bottom

Clip

Clip

Cut 2 from fashion fabric.
Cut 2 from lining fabric.
¼" seam allowances

Leave open on lining
for turning.

VELVET HANDBAG
Stitches Used

Chainstitch vine

Rosebud and leaves

Loopy Chrysanthemum

SUNFLOWER GARDEN VEST

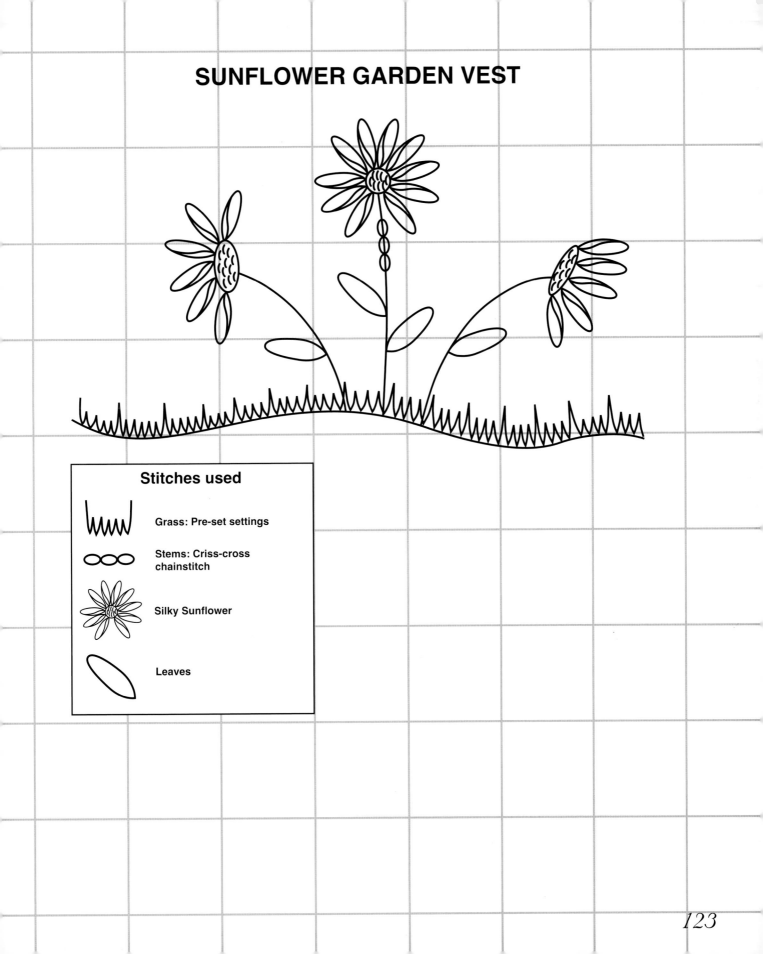

Stitches used

Grass: Pre-set settings

Stems: Criss-cross chainstitch

Silky Sunflower

Leaves

123

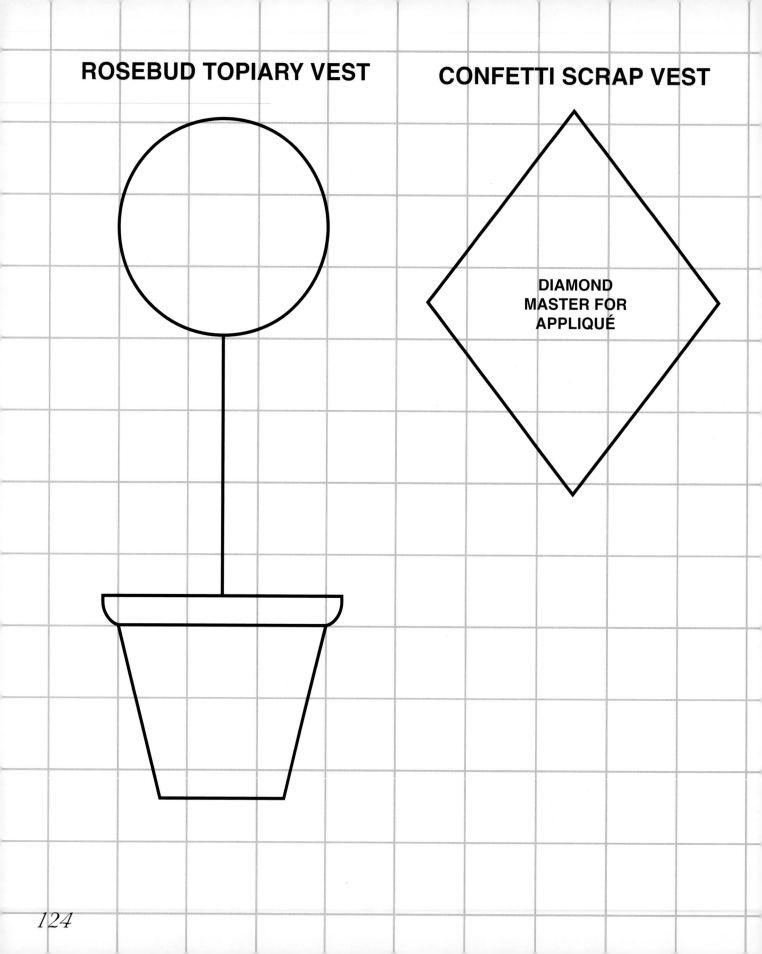

ROSEBUD TOPIARY VEST

CONFETTI SCRAP VEST

**DIAMOND
MASTER FOR
APPLIQUÉ**

INDEX